SHOTGUNS FOR WINGSHOOTING

John Barsness

Photos by John Barsness and Eileen Clarke

Published by

krause publications

The World's Largest Hobby & Collectibles Publisher

Please call or write for our free catalog. Our toll-free number to place an order or obtain a free catalog is 800-258-0929 or please use our regular business telephone 715-445-2214 for editorial comment and further information.

Library of Congress Catalog Number: 99-61455s
ISBN: 0-87341-671-6
Printed in the United States of America

DEDICATION

To Eileen, who showed me all the things that can go wrong with a shotgun, and Bob Brister, who showed me all the things that can go right.

$\mathcal{A}$CKNOWLEDGMENTS

Many thanks to the folks who helped make this book possible:

Mike Larsen and Bill Stevens of Federal

Mike Jordan and Kevin Howard of Winchester Ammunition

Mike Prosceno and Linda Blackburn of Remington

Travis Hall of Browning

Ken Levin of Bismuth

"Cuz" Strickland of Mossy Oak

Bob and Hilda Pitman and all the other folks at White Oak Plantation, Tuskegee, Alabama

Web Parton, desert quail guide extraordinaire of Oracle, Arizona

Tim Crawford and his wonderful throwing machines

Liz Lewis and her shooting instruction

Bill Heckman and his fine gunsmithing

Steven Dodd Hughes, for everything

TABLE OF CONTENTS

FOREWORD

Quite often you find a wingshooter primarily focused on one aspect of the adventure. For some it's the bond of man and working gun dog. Others relish the shotguns. For some it's keeping score and improving their shooting skills. And I've known folks who just want a reason to be in the field. For John Barsness, it is the hunt.

I want you to know John owns sidelocks and pumpguns, he's never been without a Lab, he shoots good scores and he likes to be in the field year-round. And his wife, Eileen Clarke is known far and wide as the "Queen of Game Cookery." But it is the hunt and the telling of the hunting story that fuels John Barsness.

I started noticing John's byline in quality sporting publications long before I met him. An engaging hunting story is reason enough to note the author, and many others noticed his work in such magazines as *Sports Illustrated*, *Field & Stream*, *Shooting Sportsman* and *Gray's Sporting Journal*. It was as editor of the now defunct *Game Journal* that John contacted me about writing custom gun articles for his magazine. I was flattered from the moment of introduction. His writing set a standard to reach for and his editing and suggestions stimulated my career. They still do.

With 10 minutes to peruse John's office, anyone would recognize the lair of a consummately professional outdoor writer. The large wall calendar noting deadlines, queries out, proposals, assignments and hunting trips would be the first clue. The musk ox head above his desk recalls a great tale from his big game book, *Life of the Hunt*. *Western Skies*, John's bird hunting hardback, is reflected in a sage grouse tail fan above a double gun leaning in the corner. Fly rod cases lined up like organ pipes remind me of his fishing book, *Montana Time*, and a brand new rifle scope in its new flannel wrapper, John's *Optics for Hunters*.

And books, everywhere books. Shelves of books, stacks of books, open books on top of open books on top of books with multi-colored book markers indexing esoterica. Talk to John about any book and you'll know he's read them all.

Ask John about the framed personal letters from Jack O'Connor and Elmer Kieth and you'll know he's been serious about his craft for decades.

The guns are just down the hall. On my last visit there was a raft of them. Doubles, singles, autos, pumps, bolt-actions, lever-actions, rifles, shotguns, iron sights, scopes and ivory beads. Ask John about any one of them and you'll know he's shot and/or hunted with them. If not, he'll tell you about the loads he's worked up for the weekend.

I first met Barsness at the 1989 Custom Gun Show in Reno, Nevada. He had four-wheeled all the way down from Montana in the dead of January because he wanted to see top-notch custom guns up close. (And all the hunting seasons had closed.) He is also a semi-professional stockmaker, in keeping with his hands-on approach to life, and has built some dandy walnut stocks and remodeled many others. One such stock is on his 12-gauge Fox side-by-side. It is crafted to his personal dimensions and finely hand-checkered and finished.

Last summer at an informal Sunday Schuetzenfest at a friend's place, John uncased a pump shotgun with a Holosight (whatever the hell that is?) attached to the action top. With the majority of the rest of the shooters carrying side-by-sides, John took some intense ribbing. Yet, each of us had to try this contraption that put a red circle on the same visual plane as the flying target. John's curiosity demanded he experiment with the technology. As usual, he shattered almost all of them. Some others' individual scores improved as well (not mine). Surely, not a one of us would have had the experience except for Barsness.

This is what *Shotguns for Wingshooting* is all about, sharing John's curiosity, his deep and broad knowledge of shotguns and his incurable love of the hunt. What makes this such an easy pleasure? John's voice.

The writer's voice he started looking for in his teens has been tempered with years of magazine submissions and rejections, developed by working with dozens of editors at dozens of periodicals, tested as editor of *Gray's Sporting Journal*, cemented as author of six books and is now expanding with articles in such diverse publications as *Rifle Magazine* and *National Geographic*.

John is the real deal. You can trust his gun lore, believe his ballistics, chuckle with his wit, experience his anecdotes and gain a greater understanding through his examples. Set your shotgun where you can see it. Settle the dog at your feet, let's go on an adventure, wingshooting with John Barsness.

Steven Dodd Hughes
Livingston, Montana
May, 1999

Me and Keith, my chocolate Labrador, in the sage grouse hills.

INTRODUCTION

There is something mystical about a bird hunt.

Some hunters love the solitude of a lonely hunt with a fine gun and a trusted dog. Others seem to enjoy the good-natured ribbing that comes along with a blue-collar workhorse of a gun and a dog that's heard more four-letter words than a waitress in a seaport gin mill. Though these hunters are at the opposite ends of the spectrum, they are members of the same fraternity.

But the basis of the bird hunt is the shotgun. It is a tool that craftsmen have been trying to perfect for centuries. Did the storied gunmakers of England reach the pinnacle of elegance a century ago, or is the next great idea waiting to be given form?

As a tool, the shotgun's function appears simple: The gun must bring down birds. The devilish details of this seemingly simple job have already and will continue to fill volumes. Author John Barsness adds to this pool of information with his knowledge, experience and wit as he discusses shotguns from the point of view of the job they were designed to do.

Through his years of experience, Barsness informs hunters and potential hunters on the ins and outs of which guns and loads work best for almost every game bird found in North America. Can you use the same gun for a 6-pound sage grouse and a 6-ounce mourning dove? It depends on the details, which Barsness presents masterfully with just the right mix of technical data, anecdote and wingshooting wisdom. This is a book for lovers of the gun, by one of their own. Enjoy.

Kevin Michalowski
Editor

CHAPTER ONE

THE GUN OF GRACE

In early October any latitude between the Arctic Circle and the Tropic of Cancer can be an indefinably fine place to be alive. For some humans it's even better when the air turns cool enough for a long walk where wild gamebirds live and fly. That is what we did in Montana's Gallatin Valley during last fall's pheasant season.

The cottonwood trees and brush along the stream were turning yellow and red. The sun, having lost the harsh whiteness of summer, gently touched the line of blue mountains that surrounded the valley, as if to let them know it was almost time to go to sleep. If you counted the four dogs (as any bird hunter would) nine of us would be hunting. Since the five humans all knew well the half-section of willows, barley fields and cattails along the East Gallatin River, we split up like Blackfeet surrounding a buffalo herd.

Eileen and I took our two Labradors and circled west to work the thick rosebushes and alders along the irrigation ditch. Tim, Kathy and Susan waited a little while, then called the pair of German shorthairs and started through the barley stubble toward us. It worked pretty well, too; by the time the sun touched the mountains we had several roosters.

On any good day afield there are always certain moments that become memories. Several stand out from that afternoon. The oldest shorthair, half-gray and totally deaf, had been going on point constantly, but with nothing to show for the effort but style. Just before quitting time he did it again. Tim called it a "memory point," but when I walked past him a rooster clattered up. (The ancient dog, too deaf to hear the shot, stayed on point even after the bird fell, staunch even in old age.) There is the image of Susan, when the dogs were all engaged elsewhere, running to retrieve the bird that fell into the current of the river then holding the wet pheasant and her shotgun high in each hand, tongue out of her pretty face as she panted triumphantly like a Labrador.

The moment I remember best was when the younger shorthair went on point some 300 yards across the barley field. Eileen and I heard Kathy shout, "Point!", so we turned to watch the three hunters walk up to the tiny brown statue in the pale yellow stubble. The bird rose in front of Tim and we could see him raise the little 16-gauge English gun. The pheasant fell—as it generally does when Tim shoots—half a heartbeat before we heard the shot.

"All *right*," Eileen said softly. We were just across the ditch from each other, the two Labs standing 30 yards upstream, wondering why we'd stopped hunting. Eileen is pure Irish, even if three generations removed from the old country, and loves to see wild game of any sort hit the ground. I suspect you could find more than one really predatory poacher in her family tree, eager for both the chase and a taste of wild meat.

She was still smiling as she turned toward me. "Something just struck me. You really wouldn't notice Tim walking down Main Street. I mean, he's a decent-looking but basically average guy. But when he shoots he's really graceful."

I nodded, because I had seen it before, everyone from young women to old men transformed by the act of shooting a shotgun. It is a motion and moment rarely captured on film, even the moving kind, and I cannot say exactly why. Perhaps when we see the hunt again, when we know that the shotgun will rise to the shoulder and the bird will fall, there is none of that uncertainty inherent in the chase.

There's just a touch of that momentary grace in some games, say when the quarterback sends a football down the field toward a running receiver. But a game is not the hunt. A game is an athletic contest to pass away a Saturday afternoon or prove who's best or sell millions of basketball shoes. But the hunt...

The first half-ape that stoned a bird out of the air must have been amazed. If he could do it again, and yet again, he was probably regarded as something of a god, a Stone Age version of Michael Jordan or Mark McGwire. The almost instantaneous transformation of a flying bird into food is something elemental. I mean, who can compare the chase and taste of pheasant with driving to the Colonel's to collect a mass-produced chicken? And even non-hunters cannot take their eyes from the sky when a hawk dives. Whether by hawk or stone or shotgun, a killed gamebird is still sustenance taken suddenly from the air.

All of that transforms any firearm used for wildfowling into

the gun of grace. Even a hardware-store single-barrel carves a most elegant curve in the air when put in the hands of a good wingshot. The finest shotguns are contrivances of steel and wood and precious metals that come as close to high art as any architecture. When you put a perfect combination of art and engineering into the hands of a hunter to bring a delicious meal out of the sky, then you have bridged all the ages of humanity in one graceful motion.

The first "wingshooting" was undoubtedly done with a hand-filling rock. While both prehistoric and historic hunters took birds with longbows, it was more practical and easier to catch them in nets or traps. Even the first guns were far more sensibly used to shoot birds resting on earth or water than in the air: The powder had to be lit by a fuse, and the gun could go off anytime from now until never.

Practical guns for wingshooting didn't evolve until the perfection of the flintlock in the 17th century. Anybody who has fooled around with flint-fired guns knows that pulling the trigger does not mean an instantaneous shot. But the interval between thought and shot grew short enough that the hope of bringing birds out of the air became much more realistic.

The expense of early, individually-made firearms meant that "shooting flying" was not very cost-effective. Any practical peasant out for a meal would set a snare, partly because it cost next to nothing, and partly because he wasn't allowed to own firearms. Kings and dukes did not allow arms to their serfs. So wingshooting became a rich man's sport, a reputation it still

Thunderheads in early bird season, southwestern Idaho.

holds in some quarters today, particularly in Europe.

This changed over the next 200 years, even if the reputation did not. The revolutions of the 17th and 18th centuries brought commoners the right to bear arms, but the Industrial Revolution put the fowling piece firmly into the hands of the average citizen. Soon after mass production came the percussion cap, an explosive contained in a tiny copper cup that detonated on impact. Instead of a shotgun's hammer striking flint against steel, the hammer smashed the cap and ignited the charge. This very shortly led to the cartridge, with percussion cap, powder and shot all contained in one handy unit.

For a while there was some confusion as different cartridges and firing systems competed. Many became the 8-track tapes of the shooting world, but by the last half of the 19th century, cartridges had become so standardized that shooters all over the world could buy ammunition to fit their gun, whether it was made in Italy, England or America.

During the same period "choke" was perfected. From the time of the earliest guns, shooters had been trying to increase range. With single projectiles—bullets—the revolution took place much earlier, when some German developed the spiraled grooves inside the barrel we call "rifling." But it wasn't until after the Civil War that an Englishman named William Pape and an American named Fred Kimble developed the slight constriction of the shotgun's muzzle known as choke. This tiny change kept birdshot from spreading as quickly, and so allowed hunters to kill flying birds at somewhat longer distances.

Before the invention of the choke, the only way to increase the range of shotguns was to use more shot, which meant bigger and heavier shotguns. By the 1880s choke-boring, mass production and the standardization of cartridges made lightweight, long-range shotguns affordable to every class of hunter. Some poachers still set snares on the estates of English lords, but only because gunfire would alert the gamekeeper, not because they couldn't afford their own gun.

Some shooters believe the shotgun was perfected between 1880 and 1900 in the gun shops of London and Birmingham and the fields where dukes and earls shot pheasants and partridge. Since the time of the flintlock, and even before, gunsmiths had been building firearms with two or more barrels to increase the number of shots that could be fired before reloading. In those two decades, steel replaced iron which made the higher pressures of the new smokeless powders very practical in two-barreled shotguns. Before the 18th century, France and Italy had dominated the wingshooting world, both in firearms and skill, but the height of the British Empire built not only railroads and navies, but the English game gun. The English spared no expense and perfection was the only goal.

During the same period in America the number of shots a single gun could fire was increased by ingenious machinery designed to quickly reload the same chamber of a single-barreled gun. While the British painstakingly improved the mechanically primitive design of the two-barreled gun, we mass-produced "terrible engines of destruction" (to use Oliver Winchester's phrase), guns that held a dozen cartridges in a magazine and fired them rapidly. The chambering, ejection and cocking of the gun was initially accomplished by levers and slides manipulated by the shooter. But before the turn of the century, firearms had been designed that used the power of the fired cartridge to reload the gun. All the shooter had to do was pull the trigger, again and again, as the shotgun automatically loaded itself. And so, the "autoloader" was born.

Americans produced double-barreled shotguns too, but with the dawning of the 20th century, "repeaters" started taking over the market. Why? They were much cheaper. A Sears catalog from the fall of 1900 advertises the lowest grade of Remington double-barreled shotgun for $20, about twice as much as a Winchester Model 97 pump, the first truly safe and practical hand-operated repeating shotgun. By then our abundant wild birds had been reduced by market shooting and the plowing of fields and cutting of timber, but there were still vast areas of the continent, both along the coasts and on the prairies, where wild birds could be hunted by the

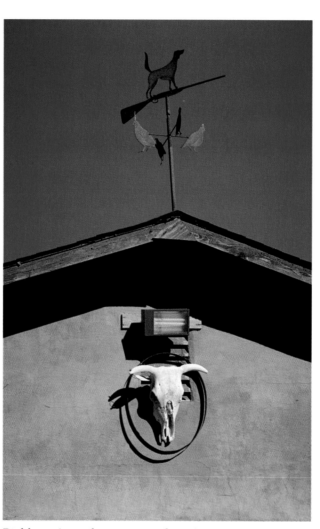

Bird-hunter's weathervane in southern Arizona.

average citizen. Those citizens saved themselves half the price of a double and bought a pump. The extra money could be used for more cartridges, to load up the buckboard with dozens more prairie chickens.

At the same time, in England and much of Europe wingshooting was still primarily a pastime of royalty, especially shooting upland birds like pheasants and partridge. (Average citizens had to make do with waterfowl hunting, since it could be done over oceans or lakes owned by no one.) While the rich royals killed as many or more pheasants than the average Nebraskan after prairie chickens, they didn't have to reload their guns themselves. Instead they carried two identical double guns, and had a peasant known as a "loader" stuffing shells into the empty gun while the marquis whacked away with its mate. Seeing no need for a gun that could shoot several shells without reloading, Britain and Europe kept building side-by-side double guns, because as long as empires and inheritances remained intact, there would always be a market for them.

In America most of our good side-by-sides had gone the way of the passenger pigeon and heath hen by World War II. They had been replaced by pumpguns and, to a lesser extent, autoloaders. Wealthier Americans still preferred their Parker or Fox doubles, and the really rich even bought English doubles. All of this added to the class distinction between double-gunners and the rest of the world. It is a distinction dating back to the French monarch Louis XIII and his 250-odd fowling flintlocks. But it did not slow the production or purchase of pumps and autoloaders.

Since World War II the side-by-side double, the gun of royalty, has grown even scarcer since modern machinery makes its vertical twin, the over-under, much cheaper to manufacture. Why buy a Winchester Model 21, the shotgun buyer of 1955 asked, when I can purchase a Browning Superposed for less than half the price? While pumpguns still sell steadily to bird hunters waiting to spend the least amount of money, in the 1950s the gas-operated autoloader was introduced, appropriately enough, by that essence of American "store goods," Sears, Roebuck and Company. Instead of using the gun's own recoil to shuck shells, the gas gun "bleeds" off a bit of the expanding powder gas in the barrel. This has the desirable side-effect of spreading recoil over a longer period, reducing felt recoil.

We can call 1900 the birth-year of the modern shotgun. By then strong steels were the metal of choice, smokeless powder was taking over the ammunition market, and all the major forms of the hunting shotguns had been introduced commercially. The period up to World War II was the time of the pump and the side-by-side; after the war came the era of the autoloader and the over-under.

License plate, southern Arizona.

All of those shotguns are still being used, and many hunters still believe that the only and best shotgun has two barrels attached horizontally. Others just as firmly believe that the finest shotguns are today's autoloaders, many using plastic stocks and aluminum frames, features that make double-gun purists slightly queasy. Somewhere in there are the pumpgunners and over-under advocates.

I love all shotguns, and shoot them all. Luckily my wife does too; right now, scattered throughout our house, Eileen and I have English, European and American side-by-sides, Japanese and European over-unders, a pile of pumpguns, and autoloaders made in the 1990s. There's even a single-shot break-action 20-gauge. We own and shoot these guns because every sporting shotgun made from 1900 to 1999 has its place in the bird hunter's world.

Unlike some of my friends, who prove the excellence of their shooting over and over again through competition, I am not really excited about shooting a shotgun unless there are feathers somewhere in the sky. One round at my local sporting clays range takes 50 shots. In researching this book, I shot the course with dozens of different shotguns. Often I'd shoot two or three rounds in a single day just to see what each gun felt like, what its strengths were and what ammunition worked best. But I always started to grow bored sometime during the second round, no matter how nifty the gun, and my scores showed it. I like to shoot clays—it beats not shooting at all—but my friend and occasional hunting partner Steven Dodd Hughes, the custom gunmaker, warned a couple of friends at lunch one day that "if you hunt with Barsness you'd better be quick, because to him each bird is a meal."

I shot my first gamebird, a hen mallard, on a lake in southwestern Montana, more than 35 years ago and over the next decade learned to shoot a shotgun by killing wild birds. By the time I saw my first clay bird the rudiments of the swing and the shot were already imbedded into my young muscles and nerves. Since then I've hunted birds from Canada to Mexico, in South America and Africa. I still think that wild birds provide the finest-tasting and most varied protein in all the world, and that any shotgun held while waiting on the edge of a marsh, carried through cornfields and sagebrush, or wrestled through briars and alders, can bring us very close to a state of grace. As a friend once said in a casual conversation, "There is hunting, and then there is wingshooting." I would only add that after wingshooting there is roast duck.

CHAPTER TWO

STOCKS, TRIGGERS AND OTHER REALLY IMPORTANT STUFF

When Americans pick up a shotgun they almost invariably raise it to their shoulder. Some do so more competently than others. Upon lowering the gun they look at the side of the barrel to see what gauge and chamber length are stamped there. These statistics can be important, though not nearly as important as two factors usually misunderstood (if not totally ignored) by the average shooter out to buy a new bird gun: the stock and the trigger.

The stock is most important, because a shotgun that fits us shoots where we look. Unlike rifles, most shotguns do not have sights. Those little beads near the muzzle don't count, unless they sit up on a heavy base or broad rib, because when shooting we see the barrel as a vague black blur, focusing on the bird, not the bead. Instead of sights, shotguns have a barrel (or barrels) and our eye.

Our eye functions as the rear sight of a shotgun, the muzzle as the front sight. This vague and optimistic arrangement works because a bird gun, by definition, sprays the sky with dozens of tiny projectiles. Remember the old saying that "close only counts in A-bombs, horseshoes and shotguns"? Because you first heard it in the 8th grade doesn't mean it's wrong. In wingshooting we are not trying to put a single bullet into a precise spot, but rather paint a piece of sky with birdshot. We often want to do it quite quickly.

This means we need to "sight-in" our shotgun as we do a rifle. By placing our cheek against the buttstock of a shotgun, we position our eye, the rear sight. If the buttstock forces us to hold our head too high, the shotgun shoots too high. If the buttstock shoves our cheek too far left, the shotgun shoots to the left. In either case our shotgun isn't sighted-in, because it doesn't fit.

The principles are that simple, but the practice more complex. The British and many Europeans have the attitude that a shotgun should be made to fit, usually by the manufacturer. With the average brand new Holland & Holland inching ever closer to $100,000, this makes a lot of sense. After all, you don't buy a $3,500 suit because the crotch of the pants hangs down around your knees. Not unless you play in the NBA, you don't.

When a prestigious British firm makes a shotgun for a customer, the prospective shooter is often fitted by the use of a "try-gun." These have adjustable stocks put together with screws so that every part can be tweaked to fit individual differences in height, arm length, facial structure, build and shooting style.

This last aspect is just as important as any other. Indeed, it's hard to tell if any shotgun fits if the shooter isn't halfway competent. This is a book about shotguns, not shooting technique, but in talking about fit some comment on practice must be made. In the past decade sporting clays has become the way to practice wingshooting, because the game was designed to simulate various shots a hunter encounters in the field. Unlike trap or skeet, where the shots are all the same whether you're shooting in Ohio or Zimbabwe, sporting clays is often called "golf with a shotgun," because every course is laid out around natural features, and the holes—excuse me, stations—differ from course to course.

Over the past five years competitive shooters have come to dominate the game and, as a result, many courses feature stations too difficult for the average bird shooter. Some of these stations are even too difficult for a lot of trick shots. My recently revised home course now has one station where two clay birds, launched from opposite directions, cross in the air. It's

There's a covey of quail under the dogs' noses, and the shot will have to be quick. Without a shotgun that fits, hitting will be difficult if not impossible.

Sporting clays has become the game for practicing wingshooting, but it may not be the best game for learning.

Some professional instruction really speeds up the process.

But most Americans don't do it that way, because, in our minds, we're natural-born Dan'l Boones and Annie Oakleys. Instead we walk into a Kmart, ask for one of them there Remington or Winchester bird guns and go shootin'. If we miss it's because of "the nut behind the barrel," not the gun. Right?

Wrong. Unlike custom English guns, the average off-the-rack American shotgun is built to fit the average American male. These do exist, but often only

a fun station, and good training for concentrating on one bird at a time. But I'd sure like to know exactly which gamebirds charge each other like Cape buffalo. It's also utterly intimidating to a beginner. So sporting clays isn't quite the practical introduction to wingshooting it was a decade ago.

Consequently a recent comment by *Outdoor Life*'s long-time shooting columnist Jim Carmichel makes a lot of sense. Jim thinks that new shooters would be better off starting with skeet rather than sporting clays. The shots do resemble short-range bird shooting (skeet was originally invented for upland practice) but since each shot is consistent and much easier than the tougher sporting stations, the beginner starts out hitting targets. This is a lot more fun than being laughed at on a sporting clays course, and hitting birds builds confidence quickly.

fleetingly. I know, because once upon a time I was that guy. In 1979 I stood 5 feet, 9 inches tall and weighed about 160 pounds. In September of that year I ordered a 12-gauge Remington Model 870 shotgun from J.C. Penney. When the local store called and said the gun had arrived, I decided to collect it after swinging by the post office. While picking up the mail I ran into a

Shooting instruction helps any shotgunner.

friend, another young freelance writer. I mentioned that I was about to pick up a new shotgun and he said, "Why gee, let's hunt some birds."

So I unpacked my brand new 870 and we were soon heading up a canyon outside of town where we'd both seen ruffed grouse. We parked his Subaru on the edge of a logging road and, while my black Labrador Gillis marked the nearest tree, loaded our guns. Very soon we both heard something moving in the brush next to the road.

"Tony, I think that's a grouse!" I whispered.

"Sure it isn't a squirrel?"

I stepped off the road. "There's one way to find out. Get the bird." I motioned Gillis into the brush and in five seconds we heard the whir of a ruffed grouse taking off. Despite our loaded guns, we really hadn't thought this through before sending in the dog. The alders and willows below the road formed an almost solid wall—except for one opening about 3 feet across. When the bird appeared in the hole I shouldered the gun and pulled the trigger. The whirring stopped, and then we heard a soft thump.

"I think I got him," I said. We wormed our way through the brush in time to see Gillis pick up a mature gray ruffed grouse. Tony told me later that he almost fainted. We'd never hunted together before, and here I was shooting grouse with a brand-new shotgun the instant I stepped out of the car.

Like all hunting, some of that shot was skill and some was luck. I knew enough about ruffed grouse to guess which way the bird might fly, but a lot of the luck lay in being average. That 870 fit me, to keep the cliché alive, like a glove. Over the next 15 years I shot it at (quite literally) tons of gamebirds, from doves to pheasants to geese, and whenever things looked right and I kept the 870 swinging, the birds went down.

But time changes all things. You can no longer order guns from J.C. Penney, and though that canyon near Missoula still holds ruffed grouse, it's off-limits to shotgun hunters. These days there are just too many picnickers, joggers and Sunday afternoon rednecks on ATV's to allow for any shooting. Which is just as well. I always figured bird hunting meant getting away from people anyway, especially people riding internal com-

A gun that fits perfectly shoots where you look. This shooter's well-fitting side-by-side breaks a "rabbit" in sporting clays.

bustion machines.

The next 20 years also changed me. I lost an inch of height and gained 40-odd pounds in weight, not all of it muscle. Then one day I found myself on the edge of a harvested cornfield, shooting doves with Bob Brister, the shooting columnist for *Field & Stream* and one of the finest all-around shotgunners in the world. I thought I was pretty impressive, since in 10 minutes all but one or two of the doves that flew across my side of the field went down.

But after watching me Bob said, "That gun doesn't fit you."

I stared at him. "What? It fits me perfectly."

He shook his head. "You're killing the birds that fly to the left pretty good, but only tailfeatherin' the ones to the right. The comb's too thick." By this he meant that the top of the buttstock was too fat, which pushed my face, and hence my eye, away from the shotgun. He could have just as well said that my face was too fat, which would have the same effect.

"No, it's not. This gun has always fit me perfectly." I raised the gun and looked down the rib.

"You're cheekin' the gun too hard. You don't do that when you shoot. Most folks don't when they shoot birds; they just raise the gun so it rests against their face. So the gun is shooting a little left. That's the reason you're nailin' those left-crossers in the head, but only getting the rear half of the those right-crossers."

Why didn't my Old Reliable fit me perfectly any more? Mostly because my face had indeed gotten fat. Since then I've lost about 15 pounds, but I'm still 20 pounds heavier than when the 870 was new. Most of us change some from 25 to 45, and from 45 to 65.

There are a bunch of ways to change the way a shotgun fits you—and unless you're about 5 feet, 9 inches and weigh around 160 pounds with "average" arm length and facial contours, you probably need to change the way a factory shotgun fits. This is why many target shotguns look a lot like try-guns.

Before going farther, let us define our terms. The critical dimensions in shotgun fit lie in the buttstock, since these determine where our eye lines up behind the barrel. The most basic is length of pull, the distance from the center of the trigger (the front trigger in two-barrel guns) to the center of the recoil pad or buttplate.

The other basic dimension is height of comb. The

"comb" is the top of the buttstock. Place a yardstick on top of the barrel so that it extends past the buttstock. Then measure the space between the straight-edge and the front of the comb (the "nose") and the top of the recoil pad (the "heel").

These are the most standardized dimensions in mass-produced shotguns. Length of pull on the aver-

Bob Brister about to shoot a duck. He's looking at the bird, not the shotgun, because he knows the shotgun fits, and when it comes to his shoulder will be pointed at the bird.

age off-the-rack American gun (and those made elsewhere for the American market) measures between 14 and 14¹/₄ inches. Drop at nose about 1¹/₂ inches, and drop at heel 2 inches. Americans don't much believe in gun-fitting because these standard dimensions work some of the time for most of us. Indeed, good shotgun shooters can bend themselves around almost any stock, consciously positioning their head just so.

But when a shotgun really fits, we just sweep the gun to our shoulder and birds fall (that is, if we don't stop the swing or raise our head). When a shotgun fits we kill more birds, which is not only good for wild Thanksgiving dinners, but makes hunting a lot more fun.

SELF-FITTING A SHOTGUN

There are bangless ways to obtain a general idea of where your factory-stocked shotgun points. One of the best is to stand in front of a mirror and quickly mount the shotgun, pointing it at your face in the mirror—first making sure, of course, that the gun is unloaded. If the gun fits, you should be looking right down the barrel at your aiming eye. If the barrel points at your left ear, some work needs to be done.

The problem with this method is that many guns don't shoot exactly where their barrels point, because at the instant of being fired, shotgun barrels bend momentarily, some bend more than others. So ultimately you must shoot the gun.

Bob Brister suggests hanging up an old bed sheet marked with a bull's eye, then standing back 30 yards or so and shooting at the bull's eye until a ragged hole appears in the sheet. The hole indicates the average center of the shotgun's pattern. Don't carefully "aim" the gun as you would a rifle. Just raise it and shoot quickly, as if shooting at a bird flying straight away.

Since I'm a Montana boy with wide-open spaces all around me, I usually test shotguns by shooting at a dry cutbank or steep snowbank. Either will show where a shotgun's hitting. Three or four quick offhand shots begin to give an idea where a gun shoots, but a dozen or more don't hurt. Remember, here we're not trying to see which shotshells work best, or how many #6 shot we can get in a 30-inch circle. Instead we're just trying to get an idea of where the gun shoots for you, not the average American. Use cheap shells and shoot at whatever distance seems right. If it's a ruffed grouse gun, 25 yards works fine, but a long-range goose gun should be tested at 40 or 50 yards.

Any initial changes should be temporary. You need to shoot the altered gun to make sure the changes work before filing, sawing or bending. If the gun shoots low, raise the comb with layers of moleskin. If the gun shoots high, build up the muzzle with black electrician's tape and pieces of cardboard.

You can also slightly alter a high- or low-shooting gun by adding or subtracting length to the end of the buttstock. The comb slopes downward toward the butt. If you lengthen the buttstock with a thicker recoil pad, your face will be a little farther back on the stock, your eye will be a little lower, and the gun will shoot lower. If you shorten the stock, the gun will shoot higher.

But there's a limit to how much shortening and lengthening you should do. Too short, and your thumb will probably bang you in the nose when then gun goes off. Too long and you'll have a hard time mount-

Shotguns used in cool weather need a shorter stock, because the shooter wears more clothes.

ing the gun quickly.

How long should the stock be? One rule of thumb is to add or subtract $1/8$ inch of stock length to the standard $14^1/4$ inches for every inch you stand over or under 5 feet, 9 inches. A shooter who stands 6 feet, 4

28

inches should shoot about a 15-inch stock, and a 5-foot shooter about a 13-inch stock.

But those are only guidelines, which probably won't work with a 280-pound Cajun chef or the average super-model. The length of your arms, the amount of muscle or fat over your shoulders, your hunting clothes—all have an effect on length of pull. A longer stock tends to point more consistently and reduces felt recoil, so you should try to shoot the longest stock you can shoulder easily. This may be longer than you think, since the best way to mount a shotgun consistently is to push it away from your body, then pull it back in. Also, a shotgun used in cool weather should be ¼ to ½ inch shorter than one used for warm-weather shooting, because extra clothing forms an extra pad on your shoulder.

A more subtle dimension is "cast," a slight sideways bend of the buttstock that allows your aiming eye to line up behind the barrel more easily. Typical is a slight bend away from a right-hand shooter, called cast-off. A bend to the left is called cast-on, which naturally makes things easier for a left-hander. Cast is measured by, again, holding a straight-edge along the barrel, then measuring from the centerline of the straight-edge to the center of the recoil pad. In most stocks cast amounts to ¼ inch or slightly more.

Most off-the-rack European guns have cast-off. Many American guns don't have any cast at all,

though more show up bent every year, including such diverse items as the Ruger Red Label 28-gauge over-under and the Remington 10-gauge autoloader. Instead of using cast, Americans tend to tilt their heads over the stock to align their eye with rib or barrel. Some shotguns have such thin combs that any cast is superfluous. This used to be more common, since most shotgun stocks were styled after the thin stocks of

muzzleloaders. But these days computerized machines shape stocks, and thicker wood means less time machining, which means more profit for the gunmaker.

All of these factors—comb height, length of pull, cast, width of comb—are interrelated. Subtly different stocks can all fit a certain shooter. I say this because in my gun rack are shotguns that vary in length of pull by $1/2$ inch or so. Some are shorter because I use them in colder weather, and while most have a little cast-off, two don't have any cast at all, because their combs are thinner. Still, every one of those guns shoots where I look, and that's the real test. (By the way, the only two guns that fit me with no change in the factory stock are my pair of 16-gauge guns, a Winchester Model 12 pump and a Beretta Silver Hawk side-by-side. The Beretta has cast-off, the Winchester doesn't. All the rest have been altered or fitted with a custom stock.)

So when you hear somebody bragging about how they had their stock fitted by some expert, so now they shoot a $14^{7}/_{16}$-inch length of pull with precisely $3/8$ inches of cast, be tolerant. Don't ask if their gun still fits when they're wearing a heavy hunting coat on a December morning, or if the film of mud on the butt is what caused them to miss that last partridge. Most of the time a professional stock fitting helps, but odds are that three different stock fitters will prescribe three slightly different sets of dimensions.

Some folks advise that an upland gun should shoot slightly high, since most upland birds flush from the ground and are rising when we shoot. A gun that throws about two-thirds of its shot above where you point thus builds a little natural lead on flushing quail, grouse or pheasants.

As Jake Barnes said in *The Sun Also Rises*, "Isn't it pretty to think so?"

Over the years I've noticed that wild birds fly in all different directions, sometimes even downhill. And when you're above the bird, any gun tends to shoot higher yet. When we shoot a shotgun we lean our head forward onto the stock, so our face tilts forward. When we point the shotgun much below level, our face ends up more perpendicular to the gun, slightly raising our eye. This doesn't matter much if, when shooting on the level, the gun shoots right where we point it. But a high-shooting gun often shoots too

If the shooter makes a quick shot, the pheasant will still be rising and a high-shooting gun might help. But if the shooter's a little slow, the pheasant's flight will have leveled off and a high-shooting gun can cause a miss.

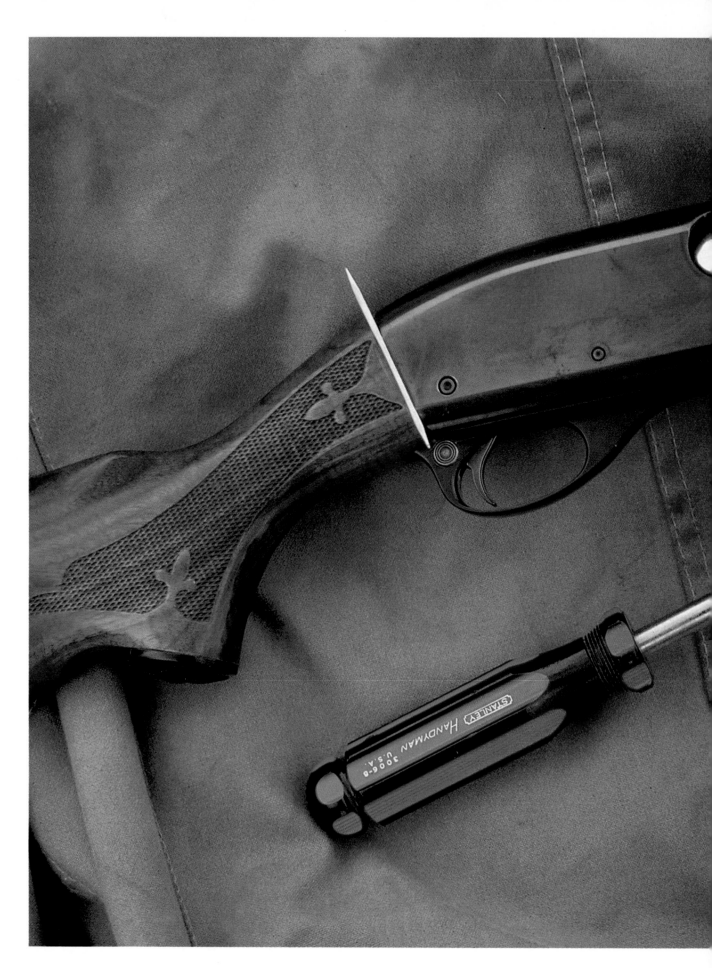

Any shotgun using a through-bolt to attach the buttstock can be easily adjusted for drop and cast. A toothpick can be inserted between stock and action to test any change before making it permanent.

33

high at birds below us, whether ducks being shot from a high bank or grouse flushing from a draw. I do have a couple of guns that shoot slightly high, no more than a few inches at 30 yards, but any new gun that shoots much higher gets altered. (It would seem logical that a shotgun should shoot low at game above us, for the opposite reason: Our head tilts even more forward, lowering our eye. But if our head tilts too far forward, we're looking at the back of the action, not down the barrel, so most of us unconsciously compensate by raising our head slightly.)

Once you've decided to make some permanent changes there are several options. Good gunsmiths can heat the thinnest part of the stock, the grip, and actually bend it. When the wood cools it stays pretty much where it was bent. Or they can fit an adjustable comb. Common in competition guns, these feature bolts that can adjust the comb horizontally and vertically, so "sighting-in" your shotgun really does resemble adjusting the rifle's rear sight. But most hunters don't like their looks.

Shotguns with a buttstock attached by a long screw through a lengthwise hole in the stock (called, aptly enough, a through-bolt) can be adjusted pretty easily. Some factory guns are even designed to be somewhat adjustable. But even if they aren't, the job's simple. This is how I fixed my 870 after that dove shoot. First I loosened the stock screw (you get to it by removing the recoil pad), then placed a toothpick between the rear of the gun's receiver and the left side of the stock. After tightening the stock screw, the buttstock angled slightly away from my face. When I cheeked the gun (naturally, not hard) I was looking right down the rib.

Then I went to my local sporting clays range and shot a round, paying particular attention to targets flying to the right. I shot a slightly better score than ever. So I went home, removed the stock entirely and, with a wood rasp, removed about a toothpick's width of wood from the right side of the stock where it butted up against the action, making the change permanent. After one more trip to the range I decided the change was a hair too much, so rasped another slight adjustment. Now the 870 shoots right where I look again. If you have a little skill with woodworking tools, this is an easy enough job on any gun with a through-bolt, which includes almost all pumps and autoloaders, and even many doubles.

You can make a shotgun shoot lower by rasping down the comb, then sanding and refinishing the wood. You can also do this on guns with synthetic stocks. Just be sure the walls are thick enough to withstand some rasping. Find out by removing the recoil pad. Shotguns also shoot lower with a higher rib, or after having a rib installed on bare barrels. One reason ventilated ribs have become almost standard on pumps and autos these days is that bare barrels tend to shoot slightly high. They have to, since the shooter is looking "downhill" from the action down along the tapered barrel.

Length of pull is easily changed. If you don't require much change, a thicker or thinner recoil pad does the job. Changes of more than $1/4$ inch or so require cutting wood off the butt, or adding a spacer between the stock and recoil pad. The first requires regrinding of the original pad, the second a new pad. But a good gunsmith can do either at minimal cost.

You can even adjust a shotgun's impact by bending the barrel—and some are indeed slightly crooked. A friend once went goose hunting with a Cree Indian guide up in Ontario. After my friend missed a few geese, the guide said the gun was shooting crooked, and suggested he could "fix it quick." My friend was suspicious, but finally said okay, since it was an inexpensive pumpgun.

Back at camp the guide cut a slot in a big stump with a chainsaw, then inserted the front half of the pump's barrel in the slot and leaned sideways on the action. He looked down the barrel once or twice, leaning on the action between looks, then handed the gun back. "Should shoot pretty good now." My friend says it's now the straightest-shooting goose gun he's ever owned, but most of us should probably trust any barrel bending to a professional gunsmith.

There are other minor factors in stock fit. "Pitch" is the angle of the recoil pad or buttplate, measured by standing the shotgun against a wall with the recoil pad flat against the floor, and the barrel against the wall. The distance between muzzle and wall is called pitch. Obviously this varies slightly with barrel length, but between $1^1/_2$ inches to $2^1/_2$ inches is normal.

Don't worry about pitch, unless the butt doesn't fit flat against your shoulder. People with heavy chests often need more pitch, say 3 inches or so, while very thin people can use zero pitch—the barrel flat against the wall when the shotgun stands firmly on its butt. A gun with too much pitch will often shoot high, because the bottom (toe) of the recoil pad pushed the gun higher during recoil, while a zero-pitch gun can have the opposite effect.

WOMEN SHOOT, TOO

Some heavy-chested men and many women shoot far more comfortably if the toe of the recoil pad angles slightly away from the pectoral muscle or breast. Many

Women make up the fastest-growing segment of hunting and shooting.

women have a very hard time with the average American stock, even if they're close to 5 feet, 9 inches, because women (in case you hadn't noticed) are built differently than men.

My wife is a good example. Eileen is only ½ inch shorter than I am but about 50 pounds lighter. This doesn't make much difference in length of pull, but as with most women, her shoulders slope more than most men's. Her face is also narrower, with higher cheekbones. According to all the rules of stock fitting her build calls for a "Monte Carlo" style buttstock, with a high comb that, behind the shooter's face, slopes rapidly down to a lower recoil pad.

Monte Carlos show up all the time on trap guns, but remain uncommon on hunting guns—I'd guess because most of us think they look weird, even though many rifles (especially those of 20 years ago) featured some variation on the theme. But most people think hunting shotguns should be stocked with straight combs. Eileen compensates (as do a lot of women and some men) by hunching her shoulders slightly when shooting.

These two stocks were custom-built to fit a shooter with a very long neck and sloping shoulders. On the left is an extreme Monte Carlo comb, on the right a more conventional design. Both have the same dimensions along the top of the comb, but different dimensions at the butt.

Women tend to be ignored by shotgun manufacturers. This is stupid, because women are the fastest growing segment of hunting and shooting folks in North America. Eileen not only takes off every fall with a bunch of her women friends for an "all-girl" bird hunt, but the last time she found an extra chunk of cash lying around, she bought an English side-by-side. The typical "women and kid's" shotguns most American gunmakers sell really tick her off. Normally these are exactly the same shotgun sold to men, but with an inch cut off the buttstock and four inches cut off the barrel.

As Eileen points out, many of today's women are as tall as the average man of two or three generations ago, when factory stock dimensions were standardized. And while cutting off a barrel may make a shotgun slightly lighter, it generally increases recoil and noise. Neither helps a new shooter. Instead, she believes one really critical stock dimension for women and kids lies in the grip.

Or rather, around the grip. Last summer she measured the hands of a bunch of women and men. Even women of "average male height" had shorter and thinner hands than average men. It's easier to hold objects that can be encircled by our grip. That's why axes and oars have handles about 4 inches in circumference, rather than as big around as a #10 can of corn. The average American shotgun measures closer to 5 inches around the grip.

This isn't a problem for most men, but to a woman or young teenager it can make a big difference. Since they can't control the grip adequately, they have to point the shotgun almost entirely with the forend hand. A firm grip with both hands also reduces kick. Since most women and kids aren't as strong as men, they simply can't control the shotgun as well, miss more, get kicked hard, and grow discouraged. None of this helps the future of shotgunning.

The noted British shooting writer Gough Thomas suggested that most grips (or "wrists" as the Brits call them) are too fat. Even for a grown man, Thomas thinks a 4$\frac{1}{8}$-inch grip is just right. This is *really* slim; you won't find too many of these even on English game guns, most of which measure 4$\frac{1}{4}$ inches to 4$\frac{3}{8}$ inches. And there are reasons for the clubby wrists of many mass-produced American guns. A stock slimmed down to 4$\frac{1}{2}$ inches or less requires strong wood, with the grain running exactly right. Most "affordable" pumpguns feature cheap (weaker) wood, and since the stock must be carved on automatic machinery, getting the grain exactly right isn't always possible. So the makers compensate with grips more appro-

priate to gorillas than soccer moms.

But would it be too much to ask for women's and kid's guns to have smaller grips? Or even to put smaller grips on some "men's" guns? I have very broad but short hands, and find a trim grip much more comfortable to carry around all day in the field.

Shotgunners argue about whether the straight or pistol grip works better. Some say the straight grip allows you to slide your hand back and forth between the two triggers of the typical side-by-side. This sounds logical, but both barrels of any decent two-trigger gun can be easily fired without moving the hand more than a tiny fraction of an inch, if at all. The rear trigger lies on the far side of the gun, positioning both triggers equally distant from the shooting hand.

According to the theorists who believe the shotgun was perfected by 1900, and that every change since only points to post-Victorian moral decay, a straight wrist brings the grip hand level with the "splinter" forend.

I've heard and read this line regurgitated by a great many shotgunners, but having considered it over the years consider it not only bullshit, but old and dry bullshit. The splinter is traditional on fine side-by-sides, but doesn't really do anything except hold the barrels onto the action. You don't grip the splinter. You grip the barrels. There's no way even the trimmest of straight grips can bring the rear hand into line with a front hand that's wrapped around the barrels. Even some British shotgunners consider the typical straight grip too straight, forcing the trigger hand to hold the gun at an awkward angle, tightening the swing. And a shotgun should swing. Maybe not like Tarzan on a vine, but it should sweep across the sky unhindered by awkward grips or moral dilemmas.

If the combination of straight grip and splinter forend is so perfect, why do many Brits slip leather-covered, spring steel "real" forends over their barrels when shooting driven pheasant and partridge? Yeah, these protect the hand from hot barrels. But if the straight-and-splinter combination points so perfectly, how can any member of the House of Lords hit a damn thing with his front hand positioned an inch lower by an add-on?

Some claim that a straight grip keeps their arm cocked higher and hence in a more consistent position. This is true—if you grip the gun tightly, constricting the swing. But the British school of game shooting suggests that a light game gun should be controlled more with the forend hand than the grip. This encourages a fluid swing with a light gun. When held by something less than a death grip, as a light bird gun

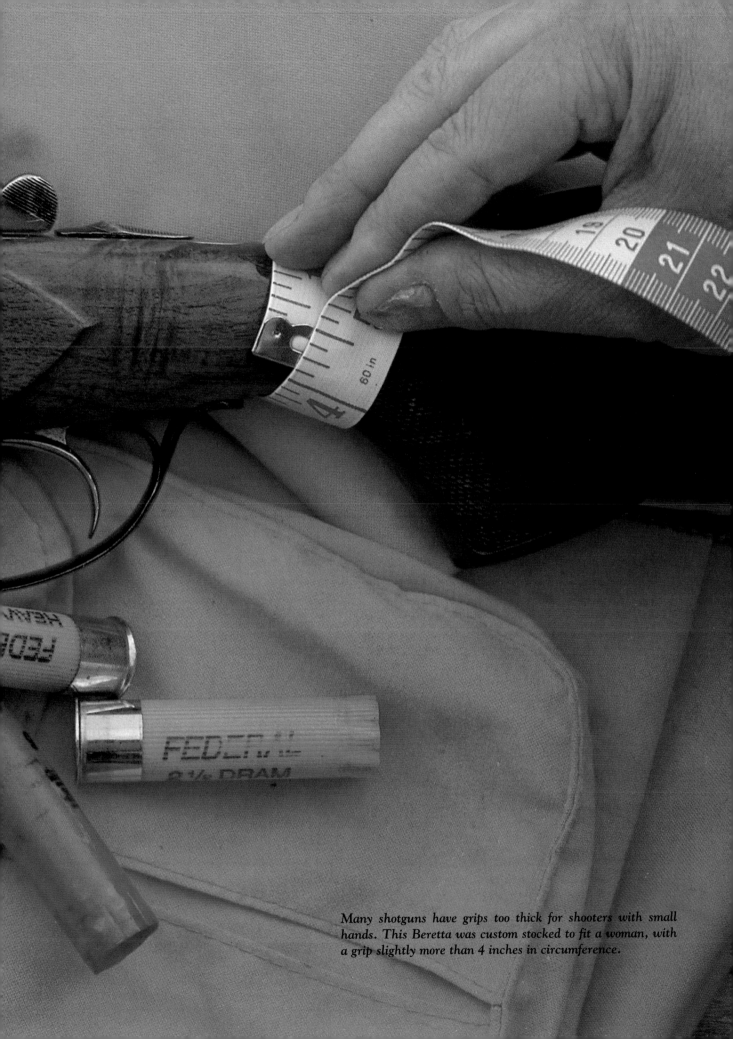

Many shotguns have grips too thick for shooters with small hands. This Beretta was custom stocked to fit a woman, with a grip slightly more than 4 inches in circumference.

should be, the trigger hand fully contacts a straight grip only with the thumb and second finger (the first finger is on the trigger). The muzzles are controlled by the forend hand which, according to much British shooting theory, should be extended well out onto the barrels.

I suspect this is the reason that a slim straight grip is traditional on light shotguns. And it's the reason straight wrists feel so quick and natural for upland shooting, where birds tend to fly off at odd angles any time they leave the ground. An extended forend hand, and light grip with the trigger hand, let us catch up to quail and ruffed grouse when they change direction.

When the shots grow longer we need bigger shotguns, both to soften hard-kicking loads and to swing smoothly on typical long-range targets like prairie pheasants and waterfowl. These guns won't change direction as well, but they will keep swinging when we need to lead a 50-yard goose a dozen feet. Big guns are tougher to hold and control, and a pistol grip helps us do both, since it allows the three non-trigger fingers of the grip hand to hold onto the gun. My own preference (which parallels that of some other experienced birdshooters) is for a straighter grip on light guns that need to be shot fast, and a pistol grip on heavier long-range guns. In between might be the perfect place for the semi-pistol grip, and indeed there is just such a grip on one of my favorite big-country upland guns, a 7-pound Fox 12-gauge side-by-side, the American "bag" grip with a rounded tip. (In Britain a semi-pistol is often furnished with a horn or metal cap and called the Prince of Wales grip.)

Another reason many Americans like the pistol grip is our preference for repeaters and over-unders with deep forends. Here the pistol grip does indeed better align our rear hand with the front hand. But a straight grip works great with light repeaters and even over-unders, as long as the forend is slim. It often is on guns under 12-gauge—in other words, typical upland guns.

But many pistol grips could be much more trim. If your trigger hand cramps up on a pheasant hunt, or your left shoulder tires during a round of sporting clays, the grip may simply be too fat. And if you prefer to hold a forend rather than the barrels of a side-by-side, try a "beavertail" forend. It is longer and fatter than the splinter, and actually meant to be gripped.

The pistol grip (top) and straight grip (bottom) help the shooter in different ways. Lighter shotguns swing better with the softer control of the straight grip, while pistol grips help control heavier guns.

My favorite upland side-by-side is that 16-gauge Beretta, fitted with a trim semi-beavertail and straight grip. (It had a pistol grip when I bought it, but after hunting with it for a while I decided to get rid of the grip. The gun feels much better now.)

According to some, combining a beavertail with a

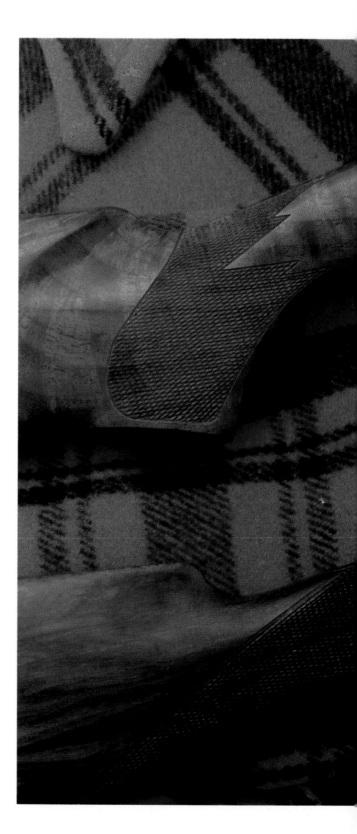

straight grip is a social faux-pas ranking alongside drinking red wine with fish. But I have seen side-by-sides made by both Purdey and Woodward (two of England's finest gunmakers) fitted with slim versions of the beavertail. I find that sort of elegant beavertail does indeed position my hands level with each other when combined with a straight grip, and keeps the forend hand well out in front, ready to chase the elusive ruffed grouse. And on dove shoots the extra wood keeps my fingertips from becoming barbecue. I also really like a good Merlot with Alaskan salmon.

You can, of course, have any shotgun restocked to

custom dimensions. But I would advise some experimentation before committing to this expensive process. It might be wiser (and cheaper) to have your stock fitted with an adjustable comb and recoil pad if you really can't hit with something close to factory dimensions.

One final possibility: Only buy guns that fit in the first place. That's what happened with both of my 16 gauges, but it's rare in American guns. A more likely source would be a shop offering both new and used shotguns, such as William Larkin Moore in California or Cape Outfitters in Missouri. The trick there is to set aside some prejudices and pick up all the guns, whether American, British, Italian, German, etc., until you find something that really fits. Since many European and British guns (and even a few American) were made to fit individuals, you'll find slight variations that might work for you. That's how Eileen found her very nice old J. Venables & Son side-by-side, a typical small-name British boxlock. Look for the gun, not the engraving or even, within reason, the gauge. For wingshooting (rather than wing-missing), you and your savings account will be much better off with a 20-gauge over-under or autoloader that fits, than an engraved sidelock 12-gauge side-by-side that does not.

Most stocks come checkered these days, even the synthetics. Checkering is supposedly functional, providing a rougher grip to help hold onto the gun. But on expensive guns it tends to become more decorative, and sometimes the exquisite little diamonds are so decorative they don't provide any grip, since to show off the stockmaker's skill they shrink to near the molecular level. Oddly enough, on many British and European guns the checkering is often not only slightly sloppy but flat-topped, neither decorative nor functional. I like good checkering—as a semi-professional stockmaker I do a lot myself—but except for wet-weather waterfowling, checkering's importance in the real world ranks alongside whether you prefer Jay Leno or David Letterman.

Much more important is what's on the butt. Perhaps you've noticed that throughout this essay I've referred mostly to recoil pads when mentioning the rear end of a shotgun. Many guns come equipped with plastic or other hard buttplates, and many British and European double guns come with unadorned (except perhaps for some mediocre checkering) wooden butts. These are all much like an icy sidewalk: slippery, and tending to hurt when they hit you.

A recoil pad not only helps ease the pain, but doesn't slide around on your shoulder when you mount the gun, or between shots. When you stand the gun in a corner it won't fall over and injure a child, or worse, a prize Labrador retriever.

Some shooters complain that a recoil pad hangs up in their armpit when they mount the gun. There are three possible reasons. One, they're mounting the gun incorrectly. As mentioned earlier, shotguns should be mounted by pushing the gun forward, then bring it back to your shoulder. Two, the stock really is too long, which sometimes happens when hunters dress in lots of warm clothes. Three, the top of the pad is too square and grabby.

The traditional solution rounds off the top of the pad. The rounded edge is then painted with varnish, or the sides of the pad are wrapped with slick tape. This works, and if the pad is black, even electrical tape doesn't look too bad. But these days you can buy recoil pads with a hard plastic insert at the top, allowing slick mounting but sticky shooting.

Some shooters, especially those with muscular or otherwise big shoulders, do fine with a relatively flat-faced pad. Slimmer shooters often shoot best with a curved pad. The slightly protruding toe and heel hold the gun more firmly in the pocket of the shoulder, making mounting more consistent and shooting more accurate.

TRIGGERS MAKE FITTING WORK

Next to the stock, the trigger is the most important part of a shotgun. What good is fitting the stock perfectly if the gun won't go bang the instant we choose? A shotgun should have a trigger much like that of a rifle, breaking cleanly with 3 or 4 pounds of pressure. Sad to say, this is rare among American factory guns, though there are exceptions.

Much lighter than 3 pounds and the gun can go off too soon, especially under the misdirection of wet or cold fingers. More than 4 pounds is too much, tending to pull all but the very heavy waterfowling guns off target. One old rule of thumb suggests that the trigger should break at about half the weight of the gun. A 6-pound shotgun should have a 3-pound trigger, a 7-pound gun a 3½-pound trigger, etc. On double guns with two triggers some suggest the front trigger should pull at 3½ pounds, the rear at 4 pounds. Supposedly this prevents the rear trigger from going off when the front trigger makes the gun go bang. But what about when the rear trigger is pulled first? The actual reason lies in leverage. It's easier to pull the rear trigger, so it feels a little lighter. Making it pull slightly heavier makes both triggers feel about the same.

All this theory cuts a little too finely for most of us,

but on any gun except perhaps a 10-gauge, I will do anything short of angering Ken Starr to obtain a clean pull of 4 pounds or a little less. If you have a cheap fishing scale you can get a fair idea of the pull on your guns. The Zebco De-Liar, in particular, is usually surprisingly accurate. Take a wire coathanger, cut off the hook, then bend the rest of the wire into short hooks at both ends, with a big half-circle curve in the middle. Hook one end around the (unloaded!) gun's trigger and hook the De-Liar to the other end. Holding the gun steady (I lay 'em down on a table) pull on the De-Liar until the gun goes click. Do this a few times while keeping a close watch on the scale and you'll have a pretty good idea of your trigger's weight of pull.

Many modern guns are unharmed by this "dry-firing" (read the manufacturer's booklet, or call their toll-free number) but older guns should have a fired case or "snap-cap" in the chamber to keep the firing pin from breaking. Snap-caps are dummy rounds with a spring-loaded button where the primer should be. They only cost a few bucks and real sporting goods stores carry a selection. Indeed, whether a shooting shop carries snap-caps is one measure of its worth.

Since I've had some gunsmith training, I often work on the triggers of my repeaters myself. But all of my double guns go to Bill Heckman, of Heckman Specialties in Livingston, Montana, and I would suggest that all of your guns with heavy triggers find their way to such a pro. Bill's not just a gunsmith but a gunmaker, who performs such tasks as re-barreling double guns—with barrels he makes himself. So he really knows what he's doing. The last gun I took in for a trigger job was my old Fox double. I specified 4-pound pulls on both triggers, and that is exactly how they came out of the shop.

A professional can also replace the factory trigger mechanism of repeaters with a totally adjustable assembly. This is more expensive than a simple adjustment, but for some guns it is worth the price, eliminating the soggy feel of many repeaters' triggers. Trigger jobs normally run $50 to $200, depending on the gun and parts. Are they worth it? You'll shoot better, especially if your gun has the typical lawsuit-designed American factory trigger pull of 6 to 8 pounds.

In much bird hunting you'll do an awful lot of walking around and very little wingshooting. As much as I love shotguns, when they aren't being shot they can turn into very ungainly objects. After two or three miles you sometimes begin to wonder how an Italian wizard can make a 6-pound *objet d'art* such a pain in the ass to carry around. A sling comes in handy at such moments, leaving your hands free for other essential tasks.

Most of my bigger shotguns are equipped with sling swivel studs of the sort used on rifles. These days many even come from the factory thus equipped, so you can sling the 10-gauge over your shoulder while hiking to the goose pit, or have the pumpgun out of your hands when you shoot two more sage grouse than your game vest will hold. And even if there's nothing else to carry, a sling makes the long hike back much more comfortable. Studies have shown that it's more tiring to carry something in our hands (or walk in heavy boots) than to carry the same load on our back or around our waists. More than once I have shot a limit of Hungarian partridge and, by the time the pickup reappeared, wished I'd remembered that fool sling.

If you don't want to screw up your vintage Parker with studs, Michaels of Oregon makes a sling with loops on both ends, designed to slip over the barrels and grip of any shotgun. Uncle Mike's also sells sets of one threaded buttstock stud and a studded forend cap for pumps and autoloaders. Unless you employ a gun bearer on a regular basis, a sling makes the wingshooting life much more livable.

BARRELS AND AMMUNITION

*S*hotguns for wingshooting are designed around a seemingly simple task: to put enough shot into the air to kill a flying bird. But the shot's trip from cartridge to bird consists of two opposing goals. First, the shot should penetrate vital areas—brain, neck, heart or lungs—which are all in the front half of the bird. Everything else being equal (which regrettably is rarely the case, even in democratic America), larger shot penetrates deeper.

One ballistician for a major ammunition company is a fan of big shot. A few years ago he designed a high-speed duck load using 1 ounce of #2 shot, containing about 95 pellets. With his pocket calculator this guy can prove that a single #2 shot will kill a duck stone dead in the air at 40 yards, because it imparts almost 4 foot-pounds of energy.

Like most waterfowl hunters I have (unintentionally) shot ducks at 40 yards, hitting them with a single #2 pellet. Sometimes I got lucky and the shot hit the head or chest, but more often the bird set its wings and sailed into distant reeds, or fell to the water and swam away. With the help of a good Labrador I retrieved many of these, and found the pellet had broken a wing or landed in the duck's intestines. Like most big-shot theorists, our ballistician forgot (or never learned, because I do not believe he has ever shot a duck) that foot-pounds do no good if they don't land in the right place.

To increase the odds that at least one pellet hits the head, neck or chest, several pellets should hit the bird. More small shot can be stuffed into any shotshell, which sometimes helps. Shoot a shotshell loaded with an ounce of #8 shot—about the smallest useful for bird hunting—at a cardboard box 40 yards away, and the box will be almost as full of holes as a screen door. That's because there are over 400 #8 pellets in an

Any wingshooting requires a compromise between pattern density and shot penetration.

ounce. Looking at the box, many hunters would be convinced that no pheasant could survive such a dense pattern.

But I have plucked pheasants recently killed with #6 shot, and found a couple of encysted 8's resting peacefully just under the skin against the rooster's pelvis. This happened because some dense hunter shot the rooster at 40 yards with a dense load of #8 shot.

So ammunition should shoot large enough shot in dense enough patterns to cleanly kill the bird we're hunting—and it should do so out of our Remington 870 pumpgun, not some computer model. How dense a pattern? Bigger birds like ducks and pheasants take up more airspace, so more shot is likely to hit them. Experienced hunters and ammo tests (on birds, not computers) agree that four or five pellets in the body will kill most larger gamebirds, while three will take smaller birds like doves and quail.

Several factors control how many shot hit a bird at any distance. Foremost is how well we shoot, but since

I hardly ever miss and you never do, let's look at the others. First comes the amount of shot in an individual cartridge. If our ballistician friend had designed a load using 1½ ounces of #2 shot, he'd have about 140 pellets flying through the air rather than 95, and the odds of killing a duck at 40 yards would rise by 50 percent.

At least in theory. Sometimes not all that extra shot ends up where the bird flies. Why? Entire books have been written about the subject: Gauge, hardness of shot, how the shot is packed into the shell, and the chamber, barrel and choke of the gun all affect the ultimate pattern, 25 or 40 or 60 yards out there.

Let's get the basic stuff out of the way, after which I shall confuse you with exceptions. A shotgun's "gauge"—the size of the hole in the barrel—is calculated by how many perfectly fitting, pure-lead balls of that diameter make a pound. Obviously, this was devised before computers grew popular, probably about

the time Shakespeare invoked the slings and arrows of outrageous fortune.

Since there are 16 ounces in a pound, a 16-gauge bore is the size of a 1-ounce sphere of lead. A 12-gauge bore measures slightly larger, equal to a ball weighing 1/12th of a pound, and a 20s bore fits a ball weighing 1/20th of a pound.

According to the standards of the firearms industry, each modern gauge has a bore diameter about like this:

10 gauge: .775"
12 gauge: .730"
16 gauge: .670"
20 gauge: .615"
28 gauge: .550"

The lone exception in modern gauges is the .410 "bore," with a barrel hole .410" in diameter. This came about when the .410 was devised from a handgun cartridge for use in shooting galleries—which is where

Shotgun shells come in various gauges and lengths. Top row: 2½-inch .410, 3-inch .410, 2¾-inch 28, 2¾-inch 20, 3-inch 20. Bottom row: 2¾-inch 16, 2¾-inch 12, 3-inch 12, 3½-inch 12, 3½-inch 10.

The shot is surrounded by old-style cardboard and felt wads, and three modern plastic shot-cups.

some hunters say it still belongs. This works out to somewhere between a 67- and 68-gauge. Except for the .410, you will find references quoting slight differences from these numbers. But as we shall see, thousandths of an inch don't mean all that much in shotgun bores.

In America, all except the 28- and 16-gauge also use cartridges that vary in length. If you look hard in enough countries and obscure gun shops, you can buy 12-gauge shells that supposedly measure 2 inches, $2^{1}/_{2}$ inches, $2^{3}/_{4}$ inches, 3 inches and $3^{1}/_{2}$ inches long. I say supposedly because if you buy a box marked $2^{3}/_{4}$ inches (the most common) and slap a ruler next to one of the rounds, you'll find it measures not $2^{3}/_{4}$ inches but about $2^{3}/_{8}$ inches. This is because $2^{3}/_{4}$ inches refers to the chamber of the shotgun, equal to the unfolded length of the shell after it's been fired.

The amount of shot in all these gauges and shell-lengths varies enormously. Today's gauges basically overlap each other in shot capacity. The .410 loads

vary from $^{1}/_{2}$ to $^{11}/_{16}$ ounce, the 28 will carry from $^{3}/_{4}$ to 1 ounce, the 20 from $^{7}/_{8}$ to $1^{1}/_{4}$ ounces, the 16 will hold from 1 to $1^{1}/_{4}$ ounces, the 12 from $^{7}/_{8}$ to 2 ounces, and the 10-gauge throws from $1^{5}/_{8}$ to $2^{1}/_{4}$ ounces.

The lead shot useful in bird hunting runs from #8 (about the size of the head of a pin) to #2 (more like a round, uncooked lentil). You can calculate the diameter of lead shot by subtracting the shot's number from .17 inches. So #8 shot is about .09 inches in diameter, just under 1/10th of an inch, the popular #6 about .11 inches, and #2 shot .15 inches. Shot above .17 inches in diameter also increases in .01-inch increments, but is arbitrarily designated BB (.18 inches), BBB (.19 inches) and T (.20 inches). All three are mostly used in steel shot loads these days. Why they couldn't have been called 22, 33 and 44, giving us a clue to their actual size, I don't know.

There are limits to the amount of shot loaded in each gauge. First, the more shot we crowd into a given shell, the taller the "shot column," the stack of shot in a cartridge. This increases pressures when the gun goes off. High pressures tend to crush the shot, both at the rear of the shell and, to a lesser extent, at the sides. These crushed shot zoom off at odd angles, or slow down, so they don't end up in the same place at the same time as the main shot charge.

We can mitigate this somewhat by making the shot harder, most commonly by alloying lead with a trace of antimony. An antimony content of 1 percent or slightly less is standard in all lead shot, helping the shot form in nice round spheres during manufacture. But shot made with 2 to 3 percent antimony is a little harder, and normally used in low to mid-price factory loads and most shot for reloading. Extra-hard shot uses anywhere from 4 to 6 percent antimony, depending on shot size. Larger shot doesn't deform as easily as small shot, so #2 shot requires less antimony than #8 to pattern tightly. Antimony levels above 6 percent may make the shot slightly harder, but above this level patterns don't improve, so 6 percent is about it.

Many shooters believe that copper or nickel plating hardens shot. Maybe slightly, especially with nickel, but the real function of plating involves its slick surface, which helps the shot flow through the barrel more fluidly, reducing deformation. Plating soft shot is largely a waste of time, since the pellets still deform under pressure.

Until the 1960s, shotshells used a combination of cardboard and felt wads—simple circles slightly larger than bore size—between the powder and shot. These kept the hot gas of burning powder from the shot, but allowed the outside of the shot column to scrape the steel bore. This didn't help patterns. But in the 1960s the plastic shot-cup was developed, and today almost all American, British and Italian shotshells use these cups. Many cheap foreign shells—and even one American manufacturer's lowest-priced line— still use cardboard and felt, which has a major effect on the manufacture of shotguns. We'll get to that shortly.

Modern plastic wads keep most of the shot from contact with the bore. They also feature a concave base of slightly less than bore diameter, which expands under the pressure of fired powder to perfectly seal the bore, and much more effectively than cardboard. In gauges above .410, shot-cups also feature a collapsible section between cup and base, easing the shot down the barrel more gently.

In addition, plastic shot-cups allow the use of "buffers"—plastic particles about the consistency of coarse corn meal—mixed with the shot to help prevent deformation. The very best ammunition uses high-antimony, plated shot mixed with a buffer.

All of this does wonders for preventing shot defor-

mation, and keeps more shot in the pattern even with a long shot column. Standard shot tends to string out after leaving the barrel, especially when loaded without buffers, instead of staying in a dense swarm. Think of a long shot-string as the Boston Marathon and the short shot-string as the finals in the Olympic 100-meter dash. In a long string a few of the fastest runners—excuse me, pellets—cross the finish line first. Then comes a clump of average shot, then the out-of-shape stragglers. The short shot-string hits the tape within a couple strides of everybody else.

There are some target shooters who prefer a long shot-string. If they misjudge the lead on a crossing target one of the erratic trailing shot may still crack the clay bird. But on gamebirds a long shot-string quite simply sucks. Remember, we're trying to put as many shot into one bird as possible. A chipped clay adds to the score, but a chipped pheasant does not normally add to the game bag, and may count against you in bird-hunter's heaven.

So despite the array of loads available in some gauges, some work better than others. In fact, some hunters feel there's a "perfect" amount of shot for each gauge: $1^{1}/_{4}$ ounces in the 12-gauge, 1 ounce in the 16-gauge, $^{7}/_{8}$ ounce in the 20 and $^{3}/_{4}$ ounce in the 28. And indeed these loads work great, even with relatively soft shot. Some shooters refer to these as "square" loads, because the height of each shot column supposedly approaches the bore size.

With typical skepticism, I decided to find out if this was true. Like many classy sounding generalities, it is not. In modern shot-cups, the theoretically ideal shot/gauge combinations all result in a shot column about an inch in height. Which means that $^{3}/_{4}$ of an ounce of shot in a 28-gauge is proportionately a much skinnier column than $1^{1}/_{4}$ ounces of shot in a 12. Far from "square," the 28s load is almost twice as tall as its .55-inch bore. In contrast, a $1^{1}/_{4}$-ounce load in a 12-gauge is only about 1.4 times as tall as its .73-inch bore. (Some references show much shorter shot columns for these loads, but they're based on bore-sized shot columns. The modern shot column is considerably smaller in diameter, since the petals in a typical shot-cup measure to .03 inches thick. So the shot column inside a modern 12-gauge shotshell is not .730″ in diameter but .670″ to .680″, about the diameter of a 16-gauge bore.)

So why does each load work so well in each gauge? Since the advent of the plastic shot-cup, shot deformed by scraping along the bore have been all but eliminated. Most deformation is caused by shot being crushed at the rear of the shot column. In all of these "perfect" loads, pellets at the rear have an inch of shot in front of them. This must be about the upper limit for minimizing shot deformation with lead of average hardness.

Which helps explain why the .410 patterns so poorly. Even the half-ounce load in the $2\frac{1}{2}$-inch shell stands 1.6 inches high, and the $\frac{11}{16}$-ounce load in the 3-inch shell is almost $2\frac{1}{2}$ inches high. If a 1-inch shot column is indeed ideal, then the .410s perfect load would be about $\frac{3}{10}$ of an ounce. (The ideal 10-gauge load would be about $1\frac{3}{8}$ ounces. But since the 10 is the largest legal gauge, used almost entirely for long range waterfowling, it's normally stuffed to the gills.)

Most shotgunners still believe that more shot in the shell means more shot in the bird. But it simply does not always work that way. Back in the 1970s I hunted geese with an old 12-gauge Winchester Model 97 pumpgun chambered for $2\frac{3}{4}$-inch shells. Down at the local sporting goods store the biggest loads stocked were Winchester Super-X's with $1\frac{1}{2}$ ounces of hard,

copper-plated #2's. This killed Canada geese dead in the air at 50 yards if I led them right.

In 1979 I bought a 12-gauge Remington 870 pump chambered for the 3-inch magnum. Boy, was I gonna surprise those 60-yard geese! Down at the same sporting goods store I bought some 3-inch loads stuffed with $1\frac{7}{8}$ ounces of shot. The brand doesn't really matter. What does matter is that they were loaded with average, unplated shot. I know this because I still have part of the box, since they didn't kill flying geese nearly as well as the lighter loads from the 97, despite the way they kicked my skinny young shoulder, because their pattern lost slightly more than half its shot in 50 yards. I found this out later (after chasing down several wounded geese) by shooting the load into butcher paper. At the same time I patterned the Winchester shells, which put 68 percent of their shot in the same 30-inch circle at 50 yards. (Yes, 50 yards. At the standard 40 yards the Super-X "short magnums"

It's not the amount of shot in the shell, but the amount of shot that reaches the bird. These geese were killed with buffered loads of #2 bismuth shot.

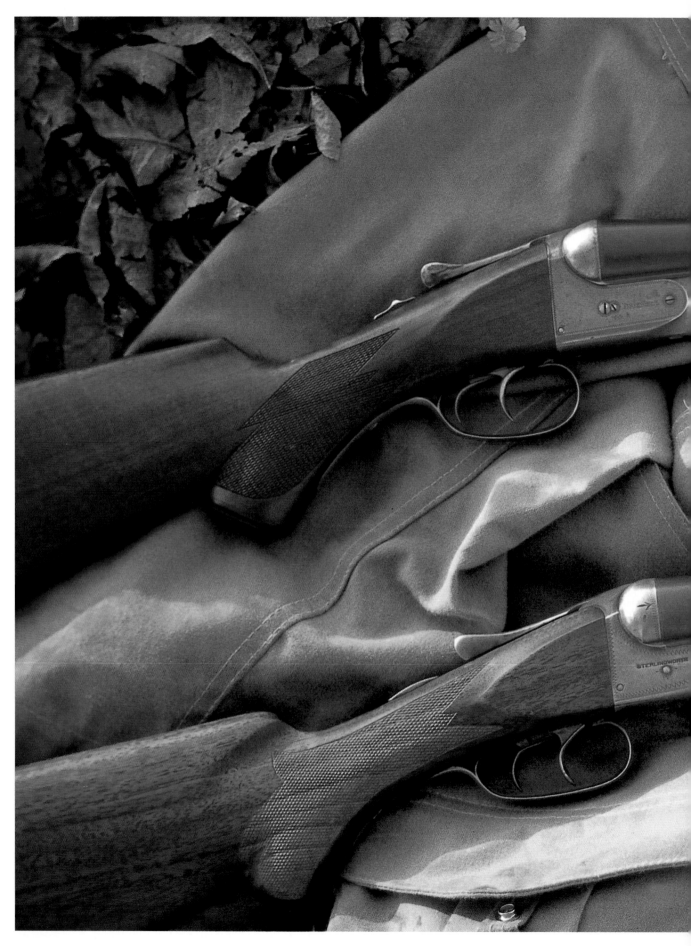

Older shotguns, like this Parker (top) and Fox, often have steep, short forcing cones designed for fiber wads. With modern ammunition, they'll kick less and pattern better if the forcing cones are lengthened.

averaged 85 percent out of the old 97.)

Let's do the math. A 1⅞-ounce load of #2 lead shot contains about 163 pellets. Patterns with my 870 at 50 yards averaged 48 percent, or about 78 pellets in a 30-inch circle. A 1½-ounce load contains 130 #2 pellets. If 68 percent hit the target, an average of 88 land in a 30-inch circle at 50 yards. The lighter loads killed better because they put 10 more #2 shot into the pattern at 50 yards.

It's an old lesson, but one many hunters never learn: What truly matters is how many pellets reach the bird, not how many live in the cartridge.

SHOT THROUGH THE BARREL

In order to reach a flying bird, the shot has to go through the barrel and choke. Here it quite literally runs into more variables. First the shot encounters the forcing cone. Since a shotshell is a plastic tube, the diameter of the shot column is smaller than the outside of the shell. So the chamber must be slightly larger than the bore. The forcing cone amounts to a funnel, easing the load's travel from the chamber to the bore.

In the days of paper and felt wads, forcing cones had to be very abrupt, often as short as ½ an inch, to prevent the thin wads from turning cockeyed before reaching the bore. With shot-cups this isn't necessary, since the plastic wad is longer than the largest bore, so it can't turn sideways. Expanding shot-cups seal the bore completely, so pressures rise abruptly when the loaded shot-cup hits a short, steep forcing cone. This deforms shot and, when the built-up pressures are suddenly released, makes the gun kick harder.

So modern shotguns typically have longer forcing cones, though most aren't as long as they should be. It takes both time and money to machine long forcing cones, so today's "affordable" American guns have cones only slightly longer than those of turn-of-the-century models. Many foreign guns are built to sell in Third World countries where fiber wads are still commonly loaded. Shotguns built in Europe, South America and the former Soviet-bloc countries often have very short forcing cones.

Consequently, one of the cheapest and best things you can do for many shotguns is have the forcing cones lengthened. Even cones 1½ inches long produce a noticeable difference in patterns and recoil, and some gunsmiths can lengthen cones up to 5 inches, not uncommon in target guns. Bill Heckman's estimate is about $50 for each chamber.

After the forcing cone, the shot hits the bore. Despite supposed standardization, bore diameters vary, too. Serious shotgunners have known for decades of the advantages of oversized bores, known as "over-

bored" or "backbored" barrels. Back in the 1930s the Burt Becker Foxes, made famous by Nash Buckingham, were overbored 12-gauge magnums. The knowledge is even more widespread among today's target shooters. You'd be hard-pressed to find a serious clay-birder whose gun isn't overbored at least .005 inches, and often .010 inches, opening the standard .730-inch 12-gauge bore to .735 inches or .740 inches. Overboring both decreases recoil and improves patterns because, as with longer forcing cones, pressures don't peak so abruptly, and fewer shot are deformed by their trip up the barrel.

These days even some manufacturers of field guns overbore their barrels. All the Ruger Red Label over-unders from 28- to 12-gauge feature overbored barrels, as does the 3½-inch magnum, 12-gauge Browning Gold autoloader. (There are undoubtedly others, but of those I am certain.) Some older guns and many foreign shotguns have undersize bores, for the same reason they have short forcing cones: ammo using fiber wads.

Because more factory guns feature overbores, the bases of many modern shot-cups have grown, particularly those in target loads. Obviously, a 12-gauge shot-cup built to expand to a .740-inch overbore will be tight in a smaller barrel.

And some of the foreign guns are very tight. For many years I shot a little XXV model AyA sidelock, a top-grade Spanish side-by-side. Then for various reasons I lost interest and my wife decided she might want the gun. So I grabbed a box of Winchester's Extra-Light 1-ounce target loads, engineered for slightly lower velocity—hence lighter recoil—than standard target loads, and we went to our local sporting clays range. Eileen yelped at the first shot, then tried another and started seriously rubbing her shoulder.

"This thing kicks like hell!" she said, not looking particularly friendly.

I shook my head. "Those loads are real light."

"So you try it." I did, and the thing kicked like hell. I tried the other 1-ounce load on hand, some Remington field loads that started faster. They kicked noticeably less, and quite acceptably.

This seemed very puzzling. According to Sir Isaac Newton, every action has an equal and opposite reaction. Slower loads should kick less.

So when we got home I turned scientific. First I measured the AyA's bores, with a Universal Shotgun Bore Gauge from Brownells, the gunsmith supply house. My model measures the bores and chokes of anything except a .410 (no great loss) down to 1/1000th of an inch. Sure enough, the bores of both barrels measured .723 inches, well under the .730-inch standard for the 12-gauge. Then I measured the wads from both loads in a micrometer. The base of the shot-cup from the Winchester target loads measured .018 inches: larger than that of the Remington field load.

Please do not generalize about Remington and Winchester shotshells from the above. Brand was not the problem. I've since measured 12-gauge wads from various manufacturers—including those two—that measured both smaller and larger. And shotgun bores vary enormously, especially in 12-gauge. In a bull session several months ago Michael Yardley, the British shotgun writer, told me he'd measured a brand new, high-grade Spanish double with .710-inch bores. Italian 12-gauge field guns also tend to have smallish bores, often around .725 inches, but their 20s tend to be oversize. Why? I'd guess most 20s go to the American market (the 12 is almost universal elsewhere) where shooters use modern shells. The bores of my two 16-gauge shotguns—a Model 12 Winchester pump and a Beretta side-by-side—measure .001 to .003 inches above .670 inches, basically right on the money.

These variations imply at least a couple of things. One, if your gun has a tight bore it may prefer the smaller wads of field ammo rather than target ammo—which many experienced hunters shoot because of its hard shot. Or, if your gun is a Ruger Red Label or Browning Gold 3½-inch or an Italian 20-gauge with an oversized barrel, it may prefer target loads. I know my own Gold autoloader functions better with target ammo than equivalent light field loads, perhaps because the bore seals better, diverting more gas to work the gun.

An off-standard bore also affects choke. Most modern American guns come with three choke tubes marked improved cylinder, modified and full. These are traditional on this side of the Atlantic, but most hunters only have a vague idea that improved cylinder creates a wider pattern, full a very tight pattern, and modified something in between. This is correct as far as it goes, but actual results vary widely from gun to gun, and there are many reasons why.

The late 1800s were the biggest period of shotgun (and other firearms) development. In the 1860s Fred Kimble developed his choke on a blackpowder muzzleloader; by the turn of the century most new shotguns fired smokeless cartridges.

But the shot inside the cartridges was still soft lead, and remained so until after World War I. So the amount of choke developed in those years became engraved in the granitic minds of most manufacturers and shooters. Over here we had the aforementioned improved cylinder (a slight amount of choke, which "improves" an unchoked, cylindrical muzzle), modified (because it was, I guess) and full, usually about .040 inches under bore size. More constriction than that, and patterns fell apart again. In Britain full choke was the same, but they called lesser chokes quarter, half and three-quarter.

Over here, improved cylinder in a 12-gauge came to mean anything from about .006 to .008 inches of constriction, modified about .012 to .015 inches. But in Britain quarter-choke was .010 inches (¼ of .040 inch), and half-choke .020 inches. So a classic British quarter-choke is not the same as the American improved cylinder, despite what you might hear. And the old British half-choke is not modified, but closer to our "improved modified," one step below full. Many Brits and target shooters, more conscious of exact choke than most hunters, speak of "points" of choke, each point being 1/1000 of an inch. So you'll hear some shooters talk about "six points in the bottom barrel, 15 in the top." This is actually the most precise way to describe a barrel's choke, but requires accurate measurement of both choke and bore.

Muzzle constriction only tells one side of choke. The other is performance, usually expressed by what percentage of a load's shot lands in a 30-inch circle at 40 yards. If a shotshell holds 200 pellets, and 100 land in that 30-inch circle, then the gun is said to shoot 50 percent patterns, about what Americans expect out of improved cylinder. Full choke supposedly produces 70 percent patterns, and modified about 60 percent. These are rough figures, for most barrels produce tighter patterns with bigger shot.

Since turn-of-the-century lead shot didn't vary much, a shooter could predict how much choke it took to produce certain results. In America, mass manufacturers simply constricted their muzzles an approximate amount and stamped improved cylinder, modified or full on the outside. We took it on faith that our gun would shoot the way it was stamped.

In Britain and Europe many guns were custom made, or choked very tightly at the factory in the expectation that the customer would have the chokes opened to whatever he desired, often with a very specific load. A double gun, for instance, might have its chokes reamed to pattern 50 percent with the right barrel and 65 percent with the left, using 1⅛ ounces of #6 shot.

But over the next 50 years ammunition changed. Shot got harder, plastic wads appeared, and these days we shoot not only lead but shot made of steel, bismuth and at least two varieties of tungsten. So what does

Like many foreign 12-gauge shotguns, this Spanish AyA has tight barrels, so tends to kick harder with the bigger wads of target ammunition.

each choke mean?

The answer to this question has grown quite complex. First and foremost, you won't know the actual constriction of your choke until you've measured both muzzle and bore. I bought my old Remington 870 pumpgun back in the dark ages before choke tubes. It came with a 30-inch full choke barrel, so for versatil-

ity I also purchased a 26-inch improved cylinder barrel. I shot the improved cylinder on short to medium-range birds like early season upland game and decoyed puddle ducks, and the full choke on late-season pheasants, sage grouse and geese.

But that improved cylinder barrel always seemed to reach farther than all the experts said it should. Late one fall I jumped a wild covey of Hungarian partridge and dropped the second bird at 40 yards. It died from a serious amount of #7½ shot. But until I bought a bore gauge the mystery of this hard-hitting barrel went unsolved.

Standard American improved cylinder constriction is about .008 inches, but it turned out that this particular barrel has a .732-inch bore and a .720-inch muzzle, for .012 inches of constriction, exactly what most American manufacturers consider modified choke in a 12-gauge. No wonder I killed 40-yard Huns, especially with handloads using hard target shot. The full choke barrel measures .733 inches with .036 inches of constriction, amounting to a slight overbore combined with an average full choke. It has always patterned almost any lead-shot ammunition beautifully.

Plastic wads have just about killed off full choke barrels with .040 inches of constriction, since modern ammo with even medium-hard lead shot will pattern 70 percent with much less choke. The full choke barrels and choke tubes of the half-dozen 12-gauge guns my wife and I own vary from .027 inches of constriction to .039 inches. The tightest is the left barrel of an L.C. Smith duck gun made in 1929, but the screw-in full choke tube that came with Eileen's 5-year-old Beretta Onyx is .037 inches smaller than the .725-inch bores. You'll find many European 12-gauge guns with tighter chokes, both fixed and tubes, for the same reason they often have short forcing cones and tight bores. Tighter chokes work better with fiber-wad ammunition.

So you don't really know your choke until it's measured, then shot. Varying ammunition causes varying patterns, even with plastic shot-cups. The cheapest ammo available from Federal, Remington and Winchester is their "promotional" stuff, often marked "Dove & Quail" or "Small Game." You'll see boxes stacked by the hundreds in sporting goods stores and discount stores every autumn, usually priced around $4 a box or even less. These normally use shot with very little antimony (though this can vary, depending on the lead market) and the Winchester stuff even uses fiber wads—though that may soon change.

Some hunters sneer at this ammunition, but it works fine for short range bird hunting, tending to pattern more widely, especially the Winchester stuff. Because of the soft shot, you often lose the outside of the shot pattern past 25 yards. This doesn't matter when shooting brush quail or ruffed grouse, but makes such ammo a poor choice for pheasants or prairie grouse.

The same companies also make mid-grade ammo with slightly more and harder shot, all using plastic wads. This ammunition patterns more tightly than the promotional loads. For the ultimate long-range performance, buy the premium or magnum loads using hard, plated shot mixed with a buffer. Yeah, they're expensive, but on late-season pheasants or other big birds they kill far better than any lesser ammo.

This variety of ammunition makes a fixed choke gun much more versatile. Shoot the cheap stuff for wider patterns at close-range birds, and the better stuff for tighter patterns at longer ranges. Just don't think you can make cheap loads work for 45-yard pheasant shooting by pushing them through a full choke. More shot deform and you may lose even more pattern than with open chokes.

If Winchester does put shot-cups in their lowest price ammunition, I will regret it. Their fiber-wad loads have always worked great for close-range shooting, and are far cheaper than the "spreader" loads on the market. These use special wads that actually separate the shot inside the cartridge, allowing it to spread more quickly. They do work, often producing improved cylinder patterns from a full choke barrel. But they tend to be expensive.

When using top-grade ammo, consider using more open chokes, even for open-country shooting. It doesn't take much choke to produce killing patterns with the best stuff. A year after I purchased that AyA, I had a gunsmith remove all the choke in the right barrel, and it produces deadly patterns with target ammo at 30 to 35 yards. My two favorite side-by-sides, a 16 and a 12, both have about .015 inches of choke in their left (tighter) barrels, a slightly tight American modified. But with premium loads using 1¼ ounces of hard, copper-plated and buffered #6 shot, both shoot patterns averaging close to 70 percent at 40 yards. The ammunition turns them into full-choke barrels, which is why when shooting lead shot I more often change ammunition than chokes.

Handloading lies a little outside the scope of this book, but let's look at it briefly. With a good manual, handloading shotshells is easy and cheap. The Lee Load-All, a simple press, can be had for $50 or less; with one you'll be able to load practice shells for under $2 a box, at the rate of three or four boxes an hour. You can simply save money, or you can handcraft ammunition you can't buy. I do more of the latter than the former. In 16-gauge you cannot buy 1-ounce loads with hard #7½ shot, or bismuth loads with #6 shot, but you can make them. If you're at all interested in handloading buy a copy of *Reloading For Shotgunners* by Fackler and McPherson (DBI Books), the best manual I've seen, and read it thoroughly before starting.

Soft lead shot tends to pattern wider, so can be useful when shooting close-range birds like these Alabama quail.

As for patterning, yeah, you can shoot hundreds of rounds at 40 yards and draw 30-inch circles around the clusters of holes, then count the holes and figure percentages for each load. But you'd better shoot at least five rounds of every load and average them, and 10 rounds is more accurate. I've obviously done some of this, and if there's a better way of ruining a day's shooting, I haven't found it. The late Gene Hill said percentage patterning was mostly for gun writers who needed something to write about. But unless you're willing to count pellets in new and interesting ways, as Bob Brister did in *Shotgunning, The Art And Science*, it's mostly a waste of time. I mean, Bob had his wife Sandy tow a boat trailer fitted with a 20-foot shotgun target past him for six months, while he whanged away at the thing. If you really want to know all about patterns, buy Bob's book. (It's out of print now but I see used copies frequently. Any full-service used bookstore should be able to locate one.)

Most of the time I pattern my shotguns more informally, and only occasionally at 40 yards, usually setting up my plywood and butcher paper at whatever range I expect to shoot birds. For close cover guns, used on birds like ruffed grouse or brush quail, I try loads at 15 to 30 yards. Shotguns used on open country birds or decoying ducks are shot at 25 to 40 yards, while long-range pheasant, sage grouse or goose guns often get tested at 50 yards or more. Then I look at the patterns and think, "Hey, that'll kill a grouse!" or "What loony-tune printed 'goose load' on the side of this box?" If you like, make little cardboard cutouts of doves, grouse, geese, etc., and place them on the pattern. Or take a standard clay pigeon and try to fit it inside the holes. These measure a little over 4 inches in diameter, about the size of the vital area of many upland birds from ruffed grouse to pheasants.

So don't count holes if you don't want to, but do evaluate how even your pattern is, especially around the edges. Tighter chokes tend to cluster shot very tightly in the center of the pattern, more sparsely around the edges. Open chokes pattern more evenly, especially "cylinder," no choke at all. You'll still occa-

Unless you know your choke's exact constriction, what's stamped on the barrel or choke tube doesn't matter. These Hungarian partridge fell at long range to a supposedly "improved cylinder" choke that was really modified.

sionally hear from barstool experts about cylinder throwing "blown" patterns, with big holes in the center. Not with modern shot cups, it doesn't.

NON-TOXIC SHOT

With non-toxic shot almost everything changes. These days we have four basic non-toxic loads available: steel, bismuth, soft tungsten and hard tungsten. (Technically these are really iron, bismuth-tin, tungsten-polymer or -matrix, and tungsten-iron, but I often find it handier to use the first terms, and suspect you will too.) Each has their own characteristics.

Steel is hard stuff, so hard that thicker wads are needed to protect the bore, and the barrel and chokes themselves need to be tougher. Since steel decelerates more quickly than lead, steel loads are typically started faster. This raises pressures, which along with the extra-hard shot is the reason you shouldn't shoot steel in Dad's old L.C. Smith, or any other shotgun not designed for steel loads. At best you'll probably "ring" the barrel right behind the choke; at worst the barrels in an old double can separate, or even burst.

Because of its light weight (about ²/₃ that of lead) steel also doesn't penetrate as well. To come close to lead shot's penetration, steel shot needs to be bigger. The rule of thumb: shot two sizes bigger than you'd normally use with lead. One and a quarter ounces of steel (about the minimum load for all-around duck shooting) fills a lot more of a shotgun shell than 1¹/₄ ounces of lead, so you also have to use bigger shells. The 3-inch 12-gauge magnum is about minimum for all-around duck shooting.

We have steel shot because on heavily hunted, shallow lakes waterfowl used to pick up lead shot while feeding, slowly poisoning themselves. But in parts of Europe lead shot is outlawed for shooting anything, and the ban has been extended to some American wildlife refuges and public hunting areas. Someday I suspect non-toxic shot will be mandatory everywhere. Perhaps not in my lifetime, or yours, but if hunting survives what passes for "civilization" these days, we won't shoot lead forever.

Steel was simply the first and easiest non-toxic substitute. It's bad for old, thin-barreled guns, but in the right shotguns steel works to medium ranges. Since the pellets are large and relatively light, when velocity drops below a certain level, steel simply doesn't penetrate adequately. That's why some hunters think

Open country implies long-range shooting, where ammunition loaded with hard shot makes a big difference, both in dense patterns and penetration.

steel works okay and other's don't. If you limit ranges to less than 35 yards, steel works fine on ducks.

But somewhere around 40 yards penetration stops like a bicyclist hitting a brick wall. The typical scenario: A drake mallard hits the water "stone dead," then rights itself a few seconds later and swims off. And just try killing him on the water. With a mallard's wings covering his body, you've got to penetrate the skull, the hardest part of a duck.

Since geese are bigger, the range can be extended somewhat with bigger shot—too big for consistent duck patterns. But beyond medium range steel pellets simply cannot match the performance of lead, even if they retain as much energy as similar-weight lead shot. They're larger, which inhibits penetration. A volleyball might be heavier than a baseball, but which will bust through a cardboard sign?

Professional ballistician Ed Lowry calls this factor "deposited energy density." (The acronym comes out to DED, singularly appropriate when rating duck-killing power.) Lowry's formula rates the DED of a #2 steel pellet at 40 yards at 1.56, while a lead #4 rates 2.30, assuming both are started at 1,330 feet per second. After shooting a number of ducks with both over the years, that seems about right.

The shortcomings of steel revived the 10-gauge. The 10 just about died after the big improvements in 3-inch 12-gauge loads in the 1960s and 70s. Since demand for the ammunition was very low, ammo companies didn't bother loading extra-hard, expensive shot in 10-gauge, let alone buffers, so the 3-inch 12 outperformed it on long-range geese. But when steel shot became mandatory, waterfowlers rediscovered the big gauge. A lot of BBB shot could be stuffed in the huge case and, since steel is so hard, it patterned quite well.

Steel also created the 3½-inch 12-gauge magnum. California is a big waterfowl hunting state, the marshes and farm fields of the central valley attracting millions of birds each year. In the California way of micro-managing almost everything, after the advent of steel the state outlawed the 10-gauge, to prevent over-eager hunters from shooting at geese at outrageous distances—"skybusting." (Evidently California hunters never do this with 12-gauge shotguns.) So the 3½-inch 12-gauge was invented to stuff 10-gauge loads into a 12-gauge shell—just as we stuffed 8-gauge loads into the 10-gauge back when the 8 was outlawed in the 1920s. Despite the super-long shot column, steel works okay in the 3½-inch 12 because it's so hard.

No matter the gauge, steel is a lot touchier than lead shot about choke. The hardness and thick wads

combining to require less choke, but exactly how much depends on shot size. This is why I broke down a few years ago and finally got a 28-inch barrel with choke tubes for my old 870, especially designed for steel shot. In the old "improved cylinder" barrel purchased with gun, some loads patterned well and some didn't. Interchangeable chokes allow certain loads to be matched to certain chokes.

The bore of the new barrel measures .726 inches, a little tight, and the chokes constrict that by .006 inches (improved cylinder), .016 inches (modified) and .036 inches (full). I also purchased an after-market choke with a constriction of .024 inches, between modified and full. For ducks over decoys the .016-inch tube works best with my favorite load of #3 steel, while the .006-inch tube does better with bigger shot.

The .024-inch tube works best with other kinds of non-toxic shot. Despite advances in steel loads over the past decade, many hunters remained fundamentally dissatisfied with its performance. Others wanted to use thin-barreled guns to hunt waterfowl, mostly classic doubles and pumps. So the search continued for non-toxic shot that worked more like lead.

The first real alternative was bismuth, a fairly heavy but brittle metal that's also a main ingredient in Pepto-Bismol. (No, bismuth shot isn't pink.) The first bismuth pellets were very brittle and irregular, but as experimentation continued it was found that a 97 percent bismuth/3 percent tin alloy worked pretty well. I started using bismuth three years ago when it became generally available, using my Federal Firearms License to order 100 rounds of 16-gauge loads and 50 rounds of 12-gauge 2's from a wholesaler. Even at my dealer's discount the 16s cost $25 for a box of 25, and the 12s $13 per 10 rounds.

The 16-gauge stuff I shot about equally at ducks and pheasants. It was a revelation, seeming to kill about like a similar load of lead. A few mallards and geese fell to the 12s, with the same results. Bismuth pellets are just slightly lighter than lead. I broke down a 1⅛-ounce 16-gauge round, finding it contained 174 pellets that averaged .13 inches in diameter. A 1¼-ounce load of lead 4's contain about 168 .13-inch pellets. So the slightly lighter bismuth allows this cartridge to carry more pellets than a heavier lead round.

A load of bismuth 2's contained 117 pellets, just about exactly the same as a 1⅜-ounce of load 2's. But they were slightly larger, running .155 inches to .16 inches rather than the nominal .15 inches of lead 2's. The difference in pellet size didn't seem to matter in the field.

By the next season Winchester started producing many of the bismuth loads. Since then I've killed a bunch of birds with the Winchester/Bismuth loads, which if anything, are a little better than the old stuff. Bismuth is about as hard as the hardest plated lead shot. Combine this with a few extra shot per ounce and bismuth patterns very well, especially in Winchester's buffered waterfowl loads.

Early bismuth tended to shatter in the forcing cone and choke, resulting in skimpier patterns in tight chokes, so some writers advised using modified or improved modified chokes rather than full. But even Winchester's unbuffered Upland loads pattern tightly in my full chokes, so that problem must have been solved. In the dozens of birds I've shot with Winchester/Bismuth, I've found only a few broken pellets. (Despite its surface hardness, bismuth shot crumbles when you accidentally bite one, so it's much friendlier to teeth than steel, or even hard lead.)

The downside? Bismuth costs at least 50 percent more than steel, load for load. But in my several seasons with bismuth I've also used fewer shells to drop each bird—and use a hell of a lot less ammo to kill crippled ducks on the water. The cost just about evens out, especially when you consider crippling. Clean kills are most important, but hunting with bismuth is a lot more fun. Why be outside the blind giving the Labrador frantic hand signals when another flock comes by to look over the decoys?

Bismuth has the head-start for use in all guns, but soft tungsten is the newest non-toxic to be approved for waterfowling. It comes in two makes: Federal's Tungsten-Polymer and Kent Cartridge's Tungsten-Matrix. Both use a mixture of tungsten (heavier than lead or bismuth) and plastic, resulting in shot exactly as heavy as lead. Like bismuth, it's soft enough to use in any shotgun.

I couldn't get any of Kent's stuff in time for real tests, and haven't yet shot any birds with the Federal stuff, but did run some range tests comparing it with steel and bismuth and the "hard tungsten" load, Federal's tungsten-iron. I have shot a bunch of this at birds too, and it's pretty strange stuff, tungsten combined at very high heat with iron in about a 2:1 ratio. It's not quite

Steel shot is required for all waterfowling today, even along streams where the hunter is just as likely to jump a pheasant as a duck.

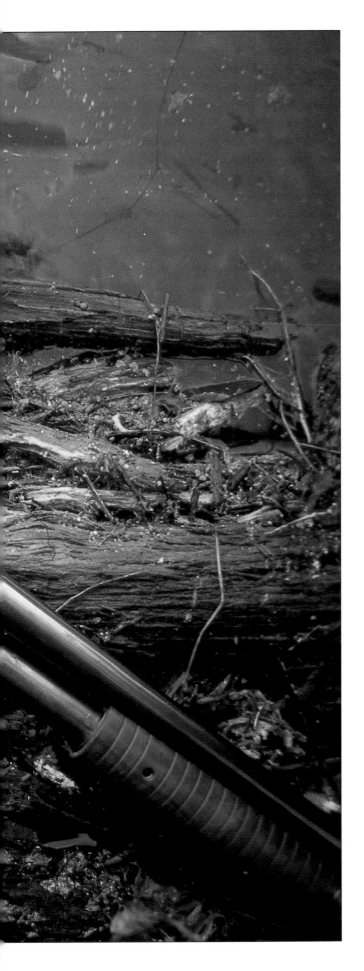

as heavy as lead or soft tungsten shot, but it's as hard as an HMO's accounting department.

In fact, it's much harder than any barrel steel. So even heavier wads must be used than with steel, which cuts down the potential shot load, and it can only be used in guns approved for steel ammunition. At first Federal tried to compensate for the light payloads by pushing the lighter loads faster, and since the shot's so hard it patterned pretty well—at least in terms of percentages. But Federal's fixation on high velocity (1,400 feet per second or more, means lots of powder) limited shot charges to $1^1/_8$-ounces in 12-gauge and $1^3/_8$ ounces in 10-gauge. Since the shot can't be made in any size smaller than #4, these simply didn't provide dense enough pattern to consistently kill ducks, even when patterning 80 to 90 percent at 40 yards.

But after tungsten-iron had been out a year or so, Federal introduced a turkey load, with more shot at standard muzzle velocities. Turkey hunters, unlike wingshooters, don't care about super speeds. Instead they demand tight patterns, in order to put lots of shot in a gobbler's head and neck.

Inadvertently this improved the hard tungsten loads for wingshooting. Federal's initial $2^3/_4$-inch 12-gauge turkey load held $1^3/_8$ ounce of #4 shot at a more normal 1,300 feet per second, versus the $1^1/_8$-ounce of their initial super-fast waterfowl load. This worked perfectly for duck hunting, so duck hunters started buying it. Federal finally got the message and now offers a full line of hard tungsten loads with closer to normal shot charges and velocities.

How do all these new non-toxics compare? I patterned and did penetration tests with Winchester's bismuth and Federal's tungsten loads, using several 12-gauge guns and a Remington SP-10 10-gauge magnum. Interchangeable chokes allowed optimum matching of choke to load. I also tested some steel loads at the same time.

Here's the deal. Both bismuth and hard tungsten patterned very well, the bismuth averaged at least 70 percent through full chokes, the hard tungsten did the same in modified chokes. The soft tungsten didn't pattern nearly as well, often only averaging 50 percent or so from some full chokes. This seemed odd, so I tore down a cartridge full of #4 shot. It was buffered, but the pellets themselves showed evidence of their plastic base, with molding rings around the middle of many pellets, and a short sprue on almost every pellet.

Bismuth shot, now loaded by Winchester, works much like lead shot on ducks, and is safe in older shotguns like this Model 97 Winchester.

Federal's Tungsten-Iron loads have gone through several changes since they were first tested in Argentina a few years ago. Present "hard tungsten" loads use more shot at standard velocities.

In other words, they're already deformed before they leave the cartridge, so they fly off at odd angles.

This isn't all bad, especially for hunters wanting to use older shotguns with tight chokes designed for soft lead shot. Right now, Federal's soft tungsten provides more open patterns in tightly-choked guns. Of course, they'll probably work on the shot until it's as round as bismuth, and patterns tightly. But right now it definitely patterns more loosely than bismuth, steel or hard tungsten.

Next came the penetration tests, performed very scientifically on old Helena, Montana phone books. By shielding parts of the books with rocks, I could try each kind of shot on a different quarter of each phone book, insuring a consistent testing medium.

Steel #2 shot (from Remington loads) penetrated about to the P's and Q's. Winchester-Bismuth 4's reached the Z's. The Federal Tungsten-Polymer 4's did about the same, except a few that exited the back of the book. Hard tungsten Federal 4's (from their original turkey load, at standard velocity) went all the way through the book and into the J's of the book behind it.

In fact, hard tungsten 4's penetrate just about as well as bismuth 2's. Unless shooting a 10-gauge, I wouldn't bother with hard tungsten 2's for any waterfowling. They don't pattern nearly as densely as the 4's, and the 4's have enough penetration and pattern for any goose that ever flew.

So which non-toxic shot is best? On a per-round basis, steel's cheapest, but I believe it's a false economy; you'll use far fewer shells of the other stuff to bag the same number of birds. Bismuth has been around longer so it's more highly perfected than Federal's soft tungsten. Bismuth is also a cheaper metal than tungsten, and there are lots of idle bismuth mines scattered around the world. If demand continues to grow, those mines will open. The price won't rise, and may even drop. At this writing, tungsten is twice as expensive as bismuth on the world market, and though the shot is mixed with cheap iron or plastic, the shells still reflect the higher price of tungsten. The difference will shrink with time, but probably never disappear.

As for effectiveness in the field, hard tungsten makes a great goose load, but for everything else bismuth and soft tungsten work as well or better, and they don't break teeth. Right now bismuth comes in every gauge, even .410, while the others offer much more limited loadings, all in 12- and 10-gauge.

SPEED KILLS

A great many experienced hunters and even some ballisticians believe that shotshell velocity doesn't matter much, since the faster you push round shot the more rapidly it slows down. A standard-velocity lead load starts at around 1,200 feet per second (fps). Add another 100 fps and you'd think the shot would still be traveling proportionately faster at say, 60 yards. But even #2 lead shot will only be going about 20 fps faster way out there. And extensive tests (my own included) have shown that shot hardness, not velocity, makes the biggest difference in penetration. With lead shot, loads starting at about 1,200 fps tend to pattern best, too.

So why push any shot faster than 1,200 fps? Good question, but there's a real reason. Fast loads mean less "forward allowance," as the British call it. Pushing shot faster does make it slow down more rapidly, but the overall time the shot spends in the air ("flight time") decreases, and a duck you might have tail-feathered is shot in the chest and head.

Some shooters say this is baloney, that the difference in a 1,200 fps load and one starting at 1,300 fps is only a few inches at 30 yards, the average upland range. I've done some computing myself and come up with about 6 inches of difference on a crossing bird flying 35 miles per hour at 30 yards. And that, gentle readers, is about the difference between a gutshot and a headshot on a ruffed grouse, or even a pheasant.

At longer ranges the difference grows noticeably. At 50 yards it's a foot or more, depending on the load and the bird's speed. Add yet another 100 fps, as with the 1,400+ of some of Federal's tungsten-iron loads, and you can really tell. Which is why when I hunt with Mike "Shoot-'Em-In-The-Head" Jordan, one of the finest wingshots I've ever seen, he usually says, at some point during the day, "Speed always helps!" This comment usually comes after head-shooting another mallard at 50 yards.

But looking for speed above all can be a mistake. Extra velocity can screw up lead-shot patterns, because the higher pressures deform more shot. This can actually reduce penetration, because the soft shot actually flattens into little discs. And as we've seen with Federal's hard tungsten, you can't sacrifice pattern density for speed. Pattern versus penetration. It's always the same old story.

But I also believe that velocities below 1,200 fps aren't so hot, except for very close-range bird hunting. Faster shot breaks bones more efficiently and, if the shot's hard enough, penetrates more deeply.

The velocities quoted are measured 3 feet from the muzzle, because with present technology it's impossible to measure speed at the muzzle. (The general estimate is a loss of 100 fps in that 3 feet.) These velocities are then translated into an obscure statistic called "drams-equivalent." This goes back to black powder days, when the stuff was ladled into shells in drams. Anybody care to tell me what the hell a dram is? Yeah, you in the back.

Yes, teacher, a dram is $1/16$ of an ounce.

Thanks, but so what? How fast do three drams of black powder push an ounce of shot?

Somebody used to know. Drams-equivalent came about because hunters accustomed to loading shells with X amount of black powder for Y power couldn't figure out the new-fangled smokeless stuff. So shotshell manufacturers printed the drams-equivalent rating on the box to guide their valued customers along the path of progress.

So why are we using drams-equivalent in Y2K? Many target shooters can translate the numbers, but most hunters have no clue, partly because drams-equivalent means different things in different gauges. In 12-gauge a $2^{1}/_{2}$-dram, 1-ounce load goes 1,100 fps, while in 20-gauge it starts at 1,165. The numbers are just as confusing and arbitrary with every other gauge and load.

Some manufacturers list simple velocities on cartridge boxes, but not many. In researching this book I shot thousands of rounds of shotgun ammunition, mostly provided by the good folks at Federal, Remington and Winchester. On those hundreds of boxes, Federal listed velocity on a few loads, mostly especially their tungsten-iron, but also some of their Premium lead. Winchester listed velocity on a single steel-shot load, and Remington not at all.

Come on, guys! This is supposed to be the Information Age. Don't drop drams-equivalent—a link to the past, and hence a large part of what hunting means to all of us. But list the darn velocity too, allowing informed customers to make intelligent choices without paging through your catalog, which the 19-year-old slacker behind the Wal-Mart counter can't find anyway. I mean, it's been more than 100 years since we started loading shotshells with smokeless powder. Let's enter the 20th century before we get too far into the 21st.

Just starting out in South Dakota.

Approximate Bore Diameters and Choke Constrictions of American Shotguns

(All Dimensions in Inches)

Gauge	Bore	Improved	Modified	Full Cylinder
10	.775	.008	.012-.015	.036+ (soft shot) .027+ (hard shot)
12	.730	.006-.009	.012-.015	.032+
16	.670	.006-.009	.012-.015	.030+
20	.615	.005-.009	.010-.012	.025+
28	.550	.005-.009	.010-.011	.023+
.410	.410	---	.010	.020

CHAPTER FOUR

DOUBLE GUNS, IN PERFECT BALANCE

The double-barreled shotgun has been held up as the ideal wingshooting tool for more than a century. Generations of Americans have lusted for doubles, because our most famous and influential shotgunning writers have long called the side-by-side and, lately, the over-under elegant, practical and, above all, perfectly balanced.

Trouble is, not one shotgunner in 100 really understands the mixture of dynamics we call "balance." Many assume that any double is a lovely thing to swing because it has two barrels, or hangs levelly when balanced on a finger underneath the hinge pin. Before we get into the differences between side-by-sides and over-unders, let's look at this marvelous balance and see what trouble we can get into.

The myth of the intrinsic balance of a double (and especially a side-by-side) began with the perfection of the British game gun in the late 19th century. I have shot and handled such guns, Purdeys and Mantons with outside hammers and Damascus barrels. Like their modern counterparts, whether made in England, Belgium, Italy or Spain, they feel as if they actually help extend the arms toward the sky.

Some whisper that this is a magical quality, its secrets found only in dusty workshops and the graying skulls of ancient craftsmen. But it is purely a matter of physics. A shotgun of any sort "balances" in several ways. The most noticeable occurs when we first lift the thing. To most of us, a lighter shotgun feels better balanced than a similar but heavier gun, because we don't have to expend as much energy getting it to our shoulder.

But even a light shotgun can feel unbalanced with too much weight distributed toward the muzzle. Thanks to the principle of leverage, a heavier muzzle makes a shotgun feel sluggish: More weight at the far end makes any object harder to lift and swing, whether a shotgun, Weed-eater or snow shovel.

So it would seem logical that a quick-pointing bird gun should be short-barreled. This is one of the greatest and most perpetuated mistakes in American shotgunning, for we must not only point the gun quickly, but swing it smoothly, at the same speed or slightly faster than the bird we intend to shoot. A too-short gun tends to swing fast, but slows down quickly, like a baseball bat held by the wrong end.

The European game gun gets around these two contradictory requirements through barrels both light and long. The barrels are filed (or "struck") toward the muzzles until very thin. This is safely possible because the pressures inside a fired shotgun's barrel rapidly drop a few inches in front of the chamber. But the thin barrels on an English gun are rarely under 28 inches in length (though we will look at exceptions later), and on a good European gun $27^5/8$ inches (70 centimeters). Thirty-inch barrels are common. This adds just enough leverage to swing smoothly, even though the whole gun may weigh six pounds or even less.

These long, light barrels, however, wouldn't swing so sweetly if the rear of the gun weighs too much. So the typical game gun has a slim buttstock, usually with a straight grip or very slight semi-pistol grip, and often the wood of the butt is hollowed out. Ideally, half the weight of the gun lies between the shooter's hands, one quarter in front of the forend hand and one quarter behind the grip hand.

All of this creates a shotgun that feels extraordinarily maneuverable, even when simply held in the hands. Like a quick-handling boat such as a dory, with its wide beam and upturned bow and stern, the heavy midsection remains stable, while the lighter ends can be turned by a flick of the oars.

In boating, the opposite of a dory is a long slim racing scull, with its entire length touching the surface of the water. While such a boat "tracks" well across open water, it doesn't turn nearly as quickly as a dory. The same is true of a shotgun with more than half its weight outside the shooter's hands. It may swing

Many shooters prefer a classic side-by-side double for all wingshooting.

The typical European-style "game gun" has long, light barrels, designed for lighter loads, while American doubles are often heavier, with shorter barrels. Typical examples seen here are (left) a German Sauer 16-gauge and (right) a Model 21 Winchester in 12-gauge.

smoothly, but doesn't come to the shoulder as quickly, or change direction as responsively.

All of this was worked out more than a century ago. It isn't magic, just physics. But it can be extremely expensive physics, because to file two barrels correctly takes highly competent hand work, and to balance the same shotgun's butt with those elegant barrels takes more hand work.

If you can't find a Holland & Holland sidelock on the used rack at the local sporting goods store, look instead for a 20- or 16-gauge pumpgun made in America before about 1960. A light Winchester Model 12 or Ithaca Model 37 from that era comes very close to the balance of a fine English double, but the closest I've ever felt was a circa-1955 Remington Wingmaster 20-gauge that appeared last fall at my local store, priced at $180. You simply cannot demand much money for pumpguns without screw-in chokes these days, but when I picked up that 6-pound, 30-inch barreled pumpgun it felt much like the fine game guns I've hefted, and for the same reasons. It had a long, slim barrel, without the excess weight of a ventilated rib, and a slim buttstock and forend. Fifty bucks says half the weight lay between my hands. I should have bought it then and there, but procrastinated. The next week it was gone, probably to be cut down for a "kid's gun." Damn!

The disadvantage of fine English and European upland guns is that this dynamic handling means the guns must be fairly light. The ideal 12-gauge game gun supposedly weighs 6½ pounds, but I have put a bunch on the scales, and find far more in the 6¾-pound range. This is still half-a-pound lighter than the average high-grade American side-by-side 12 such as a Parker or Fox, or most mass-produced 12-gauge over-unders. The downside to lightness? Real game guns can't handle high pressure shotshells, which in 12-gauge means more than 1⅛ ounces of shot. Oh, you can shoot the standard American high-velocity "duck load" of 1¼ ounces of shot, and most game guns won't blow up. But after a few hundred rounds they will start to fall apart.

The Anglophiles among us say this demonstrates that the makers of old American 12-gauge doubles and new over-unders are either ignorant peasants or reverse snobs, who either don't know the first thing about proper shotgun design, or refuse to accept European and British superiority in such matters.

This is true snobbery. There is an excellent reason why older American 12-gauge side-by-sides and modern over-unders weigh more than British game guns: They shoot heavier loads. Unlike the driven-bird shooter on the moors, the average American shotgun-ner shoots prairie grouse and waterfowl, which are pretty big and often taken at long range. And most Americans shoot at pheasants flying away, so must drive shot "right up the fundament," as a Brit might put it, and often at 45 yards, rather than at 30 yards as they fly over us like feathered Kamikaze. Fundament-shooting requires more than an ounce of shot, whether on pheasants, November prairie grouse, or flaring mallards.

This is also the reason you rarely find British side-by-sides in anything except 12-gauge. Low pressure loads in, say, 20-gauge won't even handle a full ounce of shot. So the Brits usually stick to the 12, varying the length of the shell to reproduce results similar to the smaller gauges. The standard English 12-gauge shoots loads we normally use in the 20- or 16-gauge, one to 1⅛ ounces, out of shells only 2½ inches long. When shooting lighter loads they sometimes use 12-gauge shells only 2 inches long, loaded with ¾ ounce of shot, in 5-pound guns. But even the heaviest British 12-gauge for upland shooting will weigh only 7 pounds, about like many American 20-gauge over-unders.

Why do the British do it that way? There are several good reasons. One, any shotgun tends to throw a better pattern of a given shot-charge out of a larger bore. And a larger bore allows the same velocity to be reached with lower pressures.

Another reason was suggested by Don Zutz, the late shotgun writer from Wisconsin. Since the Brits like to shoot side-by-sides with splinter (next to non-existent) forends, they have to grab the barrels instead of the wood. With the slim barrels of a 28-gauge, the fingers of your front hand can block out the view. The two fat barrels of a 12 spread the hand, providing a better look.

But over here we see the 12 as a pheasant-to-goose gauge, using anything from 2¾-inch to 3½-inch shells loaded with a minimum of 1⅛ ounces of shot, the *upper* limit for British upland loads. Consequently our 12-gauge guns tend to start at seven pounds, and we think that's pretty light. And this, I believe, is the reason Americans have long believed upland guns should have short barrels.

Especially influential on this point was Jack O'Connor, perhaps the most famous gun writer our country has ever produced. (I can think of no other whose obituary appeared in the *New York Times*.) Until his sunset years O'Connor almost exclusively shot Winchester Model 21's, the longest surviving American side-by-side. In *The Shotgun Book*, first published in the 1960s, O'Connor flatly states that a fast-handling upland double should have barrels no longer than 26 inches. This notion created a nation of shotgunners who simply would not buy an upland gun with longer barrels. And until the past decade, when screw-in chokes became universal, you couldn't buy an open-choked American over-under with barrels longer than 26 inches, because the manufacturers didn't make them.

For O'Connor and his 7-pound-plus Model 21's, this prescription was absolutely correct. I've shot several 21's of about this size, and they do handle far better with shorter barrels, because the walls of their barrels are far thicker toward the muzzles than on European-style game guns. But stick those same short barrels on a 6-pound 20-gauge and it does not swing the same way. Cut the barrels even shorter and things get real weird, at least for most adult males.

Toward the end of his life O'Connor preferred several light Spanish doubles for hunting upland game, all with short barrels. I read O'Connor a lot, and always swore that when I got over the hump as a writer, I'd treat myself to a fine double along those lines. It just so happened that when *Field & Stream* hired me as a staff writer back in the 1980s, then-editor Duncan Barnes had just such a short Spanish shotgun for sale, a 12-gauge Aguirre Y Aranzabal (AyA) sidelock, their XXV model with 25-inch barrels, patterned after British shotgunner Robert Churchill's theories about short barrels and quick "instinctive" shooting.

At the time I was living in central Montana, a land of vast valleys between islands of blue mountains. The valleys were filled with wheat fields and cattle pastures, and these were filled with Hungarian partridge. So I tested the 6¼-pound AyA on live birds, and it worked fine. It was a beautiful little thing, with gold inlays on the safety and rib, the case-hardened lockplates colored with swirls of purple and engraved in the traditional rose-and-scroll. It also had crisp, light trigger pulls, and fit me very well, with just enough cast-off. So I bought it.

It worked all right on Huns and quail, and was perhaps the finest ruffed grouse gun I've ever owned. But eventually I found it to be a lousy all-around upland gun. It started out fast, but on crossing shots was an almost total disaster, the short barrels tending to slow the instant I even thought of pulling the trigger. I eventually learned to shoot it halfway decently on short-range crossing birds, by giving the barrels a slight and very conscious push just as I shot. But my wife could shoot it much better, so now the little AyA is hers.

Why can Eileen shoot the thing, and not me? For a very simple reason. I am a 46-year-old 180-pound male who exercises regularly and, despite the belt-roll of middle age, is pretty muscular. Eileen also exercises regularly, but is a relatively tall and slim woman. Despite occasionally dragging elk quarters out of the mountains, she simply does not have my upper-body strength. So the short, light AyA does not stop dead in her hands when she gets it swinging.

Which is the reason Jack O'Connor shot well with his light, short Spanish guns. When he bought them, he was nearing 70 and did not have the strength of his younger days. He admitted as much, indirectly, in later editions of *The Shotgun Book*, by saying he preferred lighter guns as he got older. He emphasized their easy carry over the hills of Idaho, but I suspect he also shot them better than he would have a year or two earlier. The famed British shotgunner Gough Thomas also became an avid fan of the short-barreled, Churchill-style game gun late in life, and for much the same reason.

As for me, right now, Mr. Churchill can take his 25-inch barrels and put them where the moon don't shine. For most healthy males who aren't drawing Social Security, a light, short double doesn't swing as well as a light, long double. We overpower the things. Even some women have problems with them. My friend Kathy Hansen shoots a 20-gauge Parker Reproduction with 26-inch barrels. It is a classic "woman's gun," very light and short. But Kathy is a workout addict and very strong for her 5 feet, 5 inches. She shoots the Parker quickly, too quickly, most of the time, before the pattern even has a chance to open up. I suspect she'd shoot better with longer barrels.

American upland hunters who haven't fallen for the short-and-light myth are often seen staggering along under 12-gauges that weigh nearly 8 pounds, like 870 Remingtons or Browning Auto-5's or that damned Browning Superposed. Just why the 12-gauge Superposed is such a cult object among some upland gunners I will never know. It is admittedly well made, but too heavy for carrying across hill and dale. The 20-gauge model, however, is just right—with 28-inch barrels. But most American hunters have never learned there is something between a sawed-off little 20-gauge and a blunderbuss of a 12-gauge.

Just exactly where you fit into all this can only be found by shooting a few guns. We are all different in height, strength and temperament, and hunt different birds in habitat ranging from New England briars to southwestern cactus to Midwest cornfields to sagebrush plains.

Which explains why I am always suspect when some expert writes about how a 12-gauge side-by-side should weigh exactly X amount with Y length of barrels, or why a 16-gauge should weigh no more than 6 pounds, or a 28-gauge not more than 5½ pounds. Often they quote the 19th-century British gunmaker

An old Fox shotgun and some fresh mallards.

W.W. Greener, the author of *The Gun And Its Development*, one of the classic and basic texts of firearms. Greener asserted that, "The gauge and length of barrel will determine the weight of the weapon; if the weight is not proportionate to the load, it will recoil unpleasantly. A safe rule is to have the gun weigh 96 times heavier than the shot load. This means a 6-pound gun for an ounce of shot, 6³/₄ for 1¹/₈ ounce, 7¹/₂ pounds for 1¹/₄ ounce...."

Many have interpreted this to mean that a gun for 1-ounce loads should weigh exactly 6 pounds, no more and no less. Extending this logic to the ³/₄-ounce 28-gauge load means a "proper" 28 should weigh precisely 4¹/₂ pounds, and a 20-gauge using the ⁷/₈-ounce load should weigh 5¹/₄ pounds. But these folks have obviously not read Greener carefully enough (or read the quote somewhere else, out of context) for he often suggests heavier guns for the same loads, saying they handle much better. In fact, his recommendation for an all-around 12-gauge is 7 pounds, rather than the 6¹/₂ currently held up as ideal by today's game gunners.

Rather than a case-hardened law, Greener's "Rule of 96" is merely a comfortable minimum weight. For double guns it's still a pretty good rule, though I believe it can be lowered slightly with today's ammo, using cushioned shot cups and progressive powders, especially in guns with lengthened forcing cones. But beyond that minimum, any upland shooter should choose a double gun long and heavy enough to swing well in his or her shooter's hands, and one light enough to carry all day.

For my own shooting I have found a minimum of 27-inch barrels and 6 pounds to be a good rule, whether shooting a 28-gauge or a 12. And I even like a little muzzle-heaviness for much shooting out here in the open West. But that is me. I would no more presume to prescribe a 6¹/₂-pound 16-gauge with 27⁵/₈-inch barrels to you than give advice on what sort of bird dog to buy. (At least without knowing you. After that I tend to say any damn thing that pops into my head.)

Luckily we seem to be breaking away from both the too-short and too-heavy syndromes. Part of the fun of writing this book was shooting all sorts of shotguns. One of the real pleasures turned out to be Ruger Red Label 28 gauge. Now, I am not a big fan of either the 20- or 12-gauge Red Labels, though they are almost a cult in some quarters. They remind me of the 12-gauge Superposed, too heavy and sluggish, though the new straight-grip models feel much better.

But the 28 is just right, especially the option I tried, with 28-inch barrels and a very slim-wrist stock. It weighed exactly 6 pounds loaded (just what I'd hoped), had a fairly crisp trigger pull of just under 4 pounds. With a bit of cast-off and a straight comb, it fit me perfectly and handled like a dream. I would have bought it except for one little detail.

I liked the gun so much that I rushed it out to the sporting clays range without patterning a single round. It swung just as I'd hoped, easily keeping ahead of crossing targets at 35 yards or more. But by the end of the round it had me talking to myself. I'd smoke one target, then hold the same on the next and miss, or perhaps lightly puff the dust off the top of the clay without breaking it. What the hell was going on?

The next day I shot a bunch of butcher paper, which should have been done first. At 25 yards the top barrel shot right where I looked, but the bottom barrel patterned at least 15 inches high. Even with the "skeet" choke tube, the bottom of the pattern barely overlapped where I pointed.

Now, sometimes you get a cockeyed choke tube, but in this case the bottom barrel was askew. Every choke tube hit high, and in exactly the same place, which speaks well of Ruger's chokes. All of this brings us to one of the major characteristics of double guns: They must be regulated, which means they must be adjusted at the factory until both barrels put their shot in the same place.

Because of recoil, extra heavy or light loads sometimes don't overlap in the same way, but mid-power loads from both barrels should hit within a few inches of each other at 25 to 40 yards. It's surprising how often they don't, and how often the quality of the gun has nothing to do with it. Perhaps Perazzis and Purdeys always shoot both barrels into the same pattern—the few I've shot have—but I've seen almost every brand of lesser shotgun spray #6 shot into two different galaxies at 40 yards.

I do not intend to single out Ruger here, because I will own one of those 28-gauge Red Labels one day, and very soon if I have any money left over after a forthcoming bird hunt in Africa. They are fine guns, as are most Brownings, AyA's, Berettas, etc. But I have seen at least one sample of every one of those brands shoot in different places. The Ruger 28 just happened to be the only double I've shot at flying objects without patterning beforehand. This is why you should pattern every shotgun you own before directing it at a fine gamebird. They do not deserve to be wounded because of your laziness.

It would seem logical that any double with parallel barrels will shoot both to the same place, but this is simply not so. A shotgun begins to twist in recoil as soon as the shot starts down the barrel, so the right and left barrels on a side-by-side tend to shoot farther

Most shooters do better with a compromise double, neither too short and light nor too long and heavy. For all-around hunting, Steve Hughes likes his custom Fox 12-gauge, which weighs 6⅝ pounds with 28-inch barrels.

apart, and an over-under's top barrel tends to shoot higher than the lower. So the barrels must be hitched together so the bores slightly cross.

This is more easily done with an over-under than a side-by-side, one big reason over-unders tend to be cheaper. In a side-by-side the barrels must be regulated not only to converge but hit at the same elevation. And these days, choke tubes can be off, so modern regulating is double-tough, if you will allow a little pun. Unless you spend $5,000 or more, pattern your new bird gun. And even then, pattern it with several loads.

After you shoot a double, the empty shells must be removed from the chambers. The guns come equipped with either extractors, which lift the shells slightly so you can grab the rims, or ejectors, which flip the shells out like acrobats from a circus cannon. Ejectors cost more, and really have little use in most American hunting. Unless you travel regularly to South America to shoot doves, or overseas to shoot driven birds

(which means you're probably not reading this book anyway), extractors do everything needed and cost less. They also make most guns easier to open, since you're not compressing the ejector springs along with the hammer springs. If you're a reloader, you also don't have to crawl around in the grass for your empties. I prefer not to leave empty shotshells littering the landscape anyway. They aren't nearly as offensive as beer cans, but why visit the nice clean home of wild birds and leave your trash behind?

Now, on to the differences between side-by-sides and over-unders. Classically, side-by-sides are said to be more graceful, both in action and to the eye. They don't have to be opened as far to reload, possibly an advantage in a cramped duck blind.

But some shooters say they can't get used to the broad, twin sighting plane of the side-by-side. Others claim that the single sighting plane of the over-under is more precisely pointed. I tend to agree with the lat-

ter, if only because of the evidence of modern competitive shotgunning. Almost all top sporting clays, live pigeon, trap and skeet shooters who use double guns shoot over-unders.

But there are other arguments. Gough Thomas was an engineer, and had a scientific theory about side-by-sides. Some shooters have eye dominance problems. A right-handed shooter, for instance, may have a dominant left eye, or perhaps both eyes are equally dominant. Either can cause real problems in shotgun pointing. Eye dominance is a real problem for many shooters, especially women, and often grows worse in middle age. My wife went through a real trial with it in her early 40's, when for a while I never did think she'd learn to shoot a shotgun. We finally diagnosed the problem when she started shooting a compound bow. At 25 yards she'd be putting the arrows into a nice, tight group, when suddenly one would fly several feet to the left. Her left eye had suddenly kicked in, and she'd aimed with it, not her right eye.

Gough Thomas suggested that the over-under might make eye dominance problems worse, because the right eye sees the slim, single sighting plane on top of the gun, while the left eye sees the broad sides of the two barrels. Since the left eye perceives a larger image, a shooter might tend to "aim" with the wrong eye.

The theory was never tested by the great man. Instead he merely suggested it as another possible advantage of his beloved side-by-sides.

Due to the influence of Jack O'Connor, the American idea of a perfect upland gun came to be something like this 28-gauge Browning Citori with 26-inch barrels. While such guns work fine for close-range shooting, they're not ideal for all upland shooting.

Taking a high in-comer at sporting clays.

But Michael Yardley, one of Britain's top shotgun writers and instructors, has seen exactly the opposite effect during his years of teaching. In Yardley's experience, shooter's with eye dominance problems have more trouble with side-by-sides than over-unders or repeaters. Evidently the broad sighting plane confuses a non-dominant eye. This may be the real reason many shooters say they can't shoot side-by-sides.

Some shotgunners claim the over-under is stronger, hence better able to handle heavy loads. This is definitely true when the average Beretta or Browning is compared to lightweight game guns, but it's partly a matter of the particular locking system. High-quality older American side-by-sides handle heavy loads as well as most over-unders, and even some British and European side-by-sides are quite strong.

But many light game guns lock underneath the barrels, via a bolt that slides into a pair of slotted lugs in the classic Purdey arrangement. Despite its long success, mechanically the Purdey underlug locking system isn't the strongest. Far stronger (and often easier to build) is some sort of lockup at the top rear of the barrels. There are many variations on this: the doll's head of the Parker, the rotary bolt of the L.C. Smith and Fox, and the Greener crossbolt or similar Kersten fastener of German guns. No matter the particular design, they all have the same mechanical advantage over underlugs: They're farther away from the hinge

Not all doubles shoot both barrels to the same place. They should all be patterned before taken into the field.

pin, providing more leverage. Think of it this way: Which is a stronger way to lock a door, a bolt next to the knob, or a bolt in the middle of the door along the floor? The Winchester Model 21's ultra-strong action possesses the same mechanical advantage, but does it with underbolts; the hinge is simply moved farther forward.

Since over-unders must open wider to load and extract shells from the bottom barrel, most also have the hinge-pin placed farther forward. I measured the distance from the center of the hinge-pin to the bottom corner of the breech on all the doubles in the house. The side-by-sides averaged just under 2 inches, the over-unders just over 2 inches. Most over-unders use a top fastener, or locking rods extending forward from the breech into holes in the barrels, as in the Beretta. Combined with the slightly longer hinge-to-breech distance, it does seem that over-unders do have a slight mechanical strength advantage, particularly over side-by-sides using only Purdey underlugs.

You may hear about the ruggedness of the Purdey system. But even most hard-used Purdeys go back to their maker after each shooting season to be adjusted and sometimes tightened. The truth is that a good gun with a well-fitted third fastener tends to hold up longer, especially against heavier loads. I have an old Fox 12-gauge side-by-side made in 1905. It was used hard long before I bought it. One of the tests of tightness in a double involves the opening lever: If, when the shotgun is closed, the lever points slightly to the right of center, the gun has years of use left. This gun is still almost as tight as the day it left the factory, despite my own extensive use of $1^1/_4$-ounce loads on ducks and pheasants, and God knows how much shooting in the decades before it came into my hands. In contrast, I have seen many British game guns with the lever well to the left of center, despite the gun being in very good overall condition.

I do not mean to drag the classic game gun through the dirt. I love guns, especially good guns, and carrying a fine double gun makes hunting more pleasurable. But if you intend to shoot heavier American-style loads in your double, buy a gun designed for the job, whether side-by-side or over-under, not some 6-pound work of art that shoots best (and kicks far less!) with an ounce of shot.

I'm a sucker for any kind of good hunting gun, so I have owned both side-by-sides and over-unders and like them both. (I also don't have an eye dominance problem.) In general the side-by-side is prettier, but you'd be hard-pressed to find a nicer-looking little shotgun than the Weatherby Orion 20-gauge magnum my wife is trying out right now. At $6^1/_2$ pounds with 28-inch barrels, it's very trim and even the laser engraving is quite nice. And a modern 12-gauge over-under is perhaps the finest all-around shotgun in the world. I cannot imagine a better gun for the job than Eileen's Beretta Onyx. It has 3-inch chambers, which gives it enough power for anything that flies, and choke tubes in its 28-inch barrels, so it can be choked for any use. At 7 pounds it might be a little heavy for ruffed grouse and a little light for geese, but for everything else 7 pounds is close to ideal, as W.W. Greener suggested decades ago. The Onyx is also slightly muzzle heavy, because the barrels are made to withstand steel shot. That helps most of us, especially at longer ranges. Such a double will chamber and shoot ammunition made anywhere in the world, and is often the only legal shotgun in the many countries that ban repeaters. If I were limited to only one gun for everything from doves to Canada geese, this might be it.

But it only has one trigger. The single practical advantage a side-by-side has over an over-under is two triggers, since it's almost impossible to buy an over-under with anything but a single. I have nothing against the ultra-reliable modern single trigger, but it does not provide an instant choice of choke.

That's the real advantage of a double over a repeater, especially when hunting birds that usually flush singly, such as pheasants or ruffed grouse. When the bird can flush anywhere from at your feet to 40 yards from the gun, it really helps to be able to shoot with a wide-open barrel or a tight choke. Choke choice is also advantageous when waterfowling over decoys. And despite the easier-to-use barrel selectors on today's best over-unders, none allows a shooter to choose which barrel goes bang as quickly and reliably as two triggers.

Some people say they can't get the hang of two triggers. I would suggest a few rounds of skeet or sporting clays. If you aren't getting used to two triggers after whacking 100 clay birds, then go back to a single. Most people can make the adjustment.

On most covey rises there's no real advantage in instant choke choice. First you shoot a close bird with the more open barrel, then a farther bird with the tighter barrel. And on doves and geese you may not want any choice at all, instead using tighter chokes in both barrels. This is where a modern gun equipped with choke-tubes—almost always an over-under—has real advantages over the traditional fixed-choke side-by-side.

If you get into fine game guns, you'll hear a lot of talk about sidelocks and boxlocks, mostly applied to side-by-sides since, unless you're spending tens of thousands of dollars, all over-unders are boxlocks these days. The sidelock has the firing mechanism for each barrel contained on a plate that screws onto the rear of the action. The boxlock has all its mechanical works inside the action.

The sidelock usually rates as superior with real shotgun snobs, mostly because it always has. Esthetically the sidelock provides more flat steel for an engraver's art, and its lines flow more naturally into the wood of the stock. But anybody who says a fine boxlock, with fancily-filed backline and perhaps a "round" action, isn't pretty is indeed simply a snob.

The sidelock's only real mechanical advantage lies in the "interrupting sear" common to English and European sidelocks, which prevents a loaded gun from going off if dropped. But the interrupting sear isn't characteristic of all sidelocks—the American L.C. Smith comes immediately to mind—and quite a few good boxlocks feature a similar mechanism. Even

To cross or not to cross? A chukar draw in southwestern Idaho.

some over-unders such as the Ruger Red Label have a drop-proof trigger, and the Browning Gold autoloader also uses what is essentially an interrupting sear. So the drop-proof trigger isn't inherently a sidelock advantage, but a simple matter of trigger design.

Supposedly sidelocks also have triggers which are more crisp, but I've owned and shot a lot of good sidelocks and boxlocks and have never been able to perceive a real difference. A good trigger results from hard steel, honed smooth and square, not the type of lock.

The sidelock is the direct descendant of the most ancient double guns. Look at an arquebus or Kentucky rifle and you're looking at a single-barrel sidelock. Put a lock on each side of a double gun, place the hammers inside the lock, and you have a modern "hammerless" sidelock shotgun.

But the boxlock is really the ultimate evolution of the double-barreled shotgun, invented as an improvement over the sidelock. It's far simpler, and simplicity is considered a mechanical virtue anywhere outside of Germany. Because the boxlock is simple, it's cheaper to make, also considered an advantage by most humans with an income less than that of the average soap-opera starlet. The mechanism itself is more reliable, especially with modern coil springs instead of the leaf spring common to sidelocks, and mates to a stock more ruggedly. As for safety—well, let me tell you a story.

My friend John Hewitt, columnist for *Gray's Sporting Journal*, was once invited to shoot bobwhite quail on a very exclusive Southern plantation. These were wild quail, which just shows how exclusive the place really was, since these days 95% of the quail shot south of the Mason-Dixon line are raised in pens. Despite his fancy job, John is a plain man, raised in Kansas and living in Alaska, who mostly uses pumpguns. He was informed that his Model 12 Winchester pump would not do, that only double guns were allowed. So he borrowed one and went out to rub shoulders and shotshells with the rich.

One of the other invitees was a young woman. When the dogs went on point, John and this young woman were designated shooting partners. John had already loaded the chambers of his borrowed gun and was standing there, gun broken, waiting for this young woman to load her sidelock 28-gauge. This she did, then closed it with her finger on the trigger, at which point some 300-odd #8 pellets put a hole in the ground right between John's feet. He says that after a lifetime of hunting around pumps and autoloaders, that is the closest he's ever come to getting shot.

Undoubtedly an interrupting sear does prevent a few

Over-unders must open more widely to load a cartridge into the bottom barrel. This tends to make their actions longer from breech to hinge-pin, providing a little extra strength through leverage.

accidental deaths each year, though probably fewer than the number of hunters killed by lightning, snake-bite or grizzly bears. Some shooters also claim that a double gun is intrinsically safer than any repeater because it can be loaded and unloaded instantly, and when opened is absolutely safe, even with the chambers loaded. I firmly believe—and know John Hewitt agrees—that gun safety lies not with interrupting sears, but between the ears.

If you decide on a side-by-side, you'll likely be looking at the used market. There isn't space here to describe every aspect of buying used double guns, but there are a lot available right now. The prices are pretty affordable, too. Even English shotguns, since British gun laws make owning even a bird gun more difficult each year. (Evidently many London gang-bangers use Purdeys for drive-by shootings.) Consequently, you can pick up a good boxlock, particularly a non-ejector, for about the price you'd pay for a new over-under Beretta or Browning.

Whether you buy one of these, a European gun, or an older American like a Fox or Parker, watch for short chambers. Many older guns have shorter chambers than the standards of today. The most common

length in British guns is 2½ inches, but you may run into 2⅝-inch chambers in American guns, or even pre-World War I English guns. The smaller gauges have their own strange lengths, such as 2⁹/₁₆ inches in 16-gauge.

Any of these may develop higher pressures when fired with modern 2¾-inch ammunition. I emphasize may, because my friends in the ammo business have tested lots of ammo in short chambers and often find no problem. But sometimes they do, and since you have no way of testing, there are two ways to safely get around short chambers.

One is to use short ammo. This is available commercially, though at higher cost and mostly on special order. Beware, however, that with the recent high demand for short shells, some have been found to unfold to 2⅝ inches and even 2¾ inches. So there's some poor quality control going around, or outright deception. Some recent reloading manuals also list low-pressure for handloading short shells, which can be made by trimming 2¾-inch empties.

Or you can have the gun rechambered for longer shells. Some regard this as tantamount to air-brushing an Arizona sunset on a Rolls-Royce, and I'd never do

The real advantage of the classic side-by-side shotgun lies in the instant choice of chokes provided by two triggers.

The strength of a side-by-side double varies with the locking system. While both of these light 12-gauge doubles use the standard Purdey underbolt (its locking notch visible underneath the rear of the barrels) the top gun also has a Greener crossbolt, which fits into the hole through the extension at the rear of the barrels.

it to a truly valuable old gun, such as a high-grade Parker or Purdey. Many also advise that a rechambered British or European gun is "out of proof." Over there, each country has its own proof house, where new guns are fired with overloads to make sure they're safe. Rechambering negates this proof. Many shooters refuse to buy a rechambered gun that hasn't been sent back overseas for reproof, a process that can cost $1,000. (In America the individual manufacturers test each gun, which to true believers in foreign doubles shooters is simply not the word of God. Mostly, foreign proof consists of shooting one over-pressure shell in each chamber. American manufacturers do the same thing, and often repeatedly, but do not have a coat-of-arms stamp.)

If you do rechamber a light game gun, you should still shoot only light loads. My friend Layne Simpson, the gun writer from South Carolina, recently bought an old Westley Richards 20-gauge boxlock, a $5\frac{1}{2}$-pound gun. Layne had the chambers lengthened to $2\frac{3}{4}$ inches, but shoots only $\frac{3}{4}$-ounce loads at pressures well under 10,000 pounds per square inch, rather than the 13,000 pounds of some modern 20-gauge loads. This allows the use of cheap American cases, while remaining perfectly safe. What the little gun amounts to, Layne says, is a bigger-bored 28-gauge.

It's probably a good idea not to rechamber a really light ($6\frac{1}{2}$ pounds or under) 12-gauge, or even lengthen the forcing cones. Super-light guns become light by having steel pared away not just at the muzzles but around the chamber end of the barrels. And it's also probably not a good idea to trust the job to the neighborhood gunsmith. But many guns have enough steel to be perfectly safe with longer chambers. Two examples are my wife's J. Venables & Son boxlock, and my Fox Sterlingworth.

The Venables was built in Oxford, England before World War I, and is W.W. Greener's idea of an all-around 12-gauge, weighing 7 pounds with 30-inch barrels. In addition to the standard Purdey underlugs it has a Greener crossbolt, and the breech is somewhat heavier than on many game guns. Bill Heckman made some measurements, among other things finding that it had $2\frac{5}{8}$-inch chambers, which according to some sources were common before the first World War. (The Brits standardized $2\frac{1}{2}$-inch chambers during the war, reducing their standard 12-gauge load from $1\frac{1}{8}$ ounces to $1\frac{1}{16}$, to save lead for .303 military bullets.) In addition, the bores had never been repolished, common on old guns, which thins the barrels. Lengthening the chambers to $2\frac{3}{4}$ inches would bring the front of the chambers about .002 inches closer to the

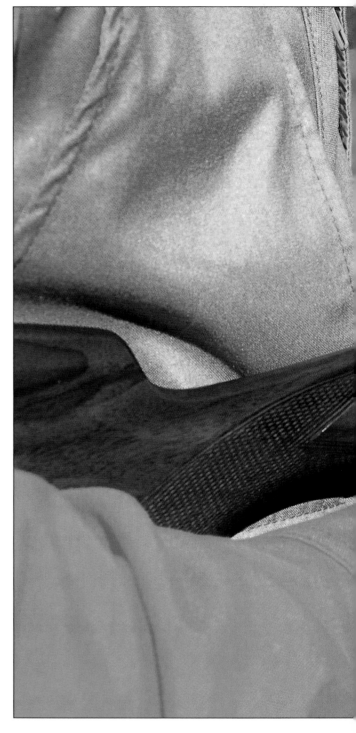

outside of the barrels, about the thickness of the page you're reading. Bill suggested that if 2/1000ths of an inch made this fairly heavy gun unsafe, then most office buildings were in imminent danger of collapse. So we did it, but did not send the gun back to England to be reproofed. But we don't shoot $1\frac{1}{4}$-ounce duck loads in it, either.

The Fox was even more of the same, also 7 pounds but originally designed for duck shooting. It also had $2\frac{5}{8}$-inch chambers, but the barrels are 2 inches shorter

On covey birds there's usually no advantage in an instant choice of choke. For bobwhite quail, this shooter chose a single-triggered Browning Superposed in 20-gauge, a light and quick-pointing upland gun.

and even heavier-walled than the Venables'. It works great with 1¼-ounce duck loads, since it was meant to shoot them in the first place. Use some judgement and you won't have any problems.

When you start looking at older doubles, you'll also encounter Damascus barrels. These were made by twisting rods of iron and steel, then welding them around a bar to form a barrel. The standard advice says they blow up, so leave the damn things alone. If you don't know anything about Damascus that's good advice, especially with cheaper guns. But many old Damascus guns are alive and working today, either British guns shot with black powder shells (still available in England) or reproofed with modern loads, or with the barrels or chambers sleeved with modern steel. Damascus isn't dead, it's just a specialty item. Learn about it if the old guns appeal to you. The patterns of old Damascus barrels can be as beautiful as intricate cobblestone streets, and just as evocative of another time and place.

Just avoid the guns like the old Pieper double my friend Jay Rightnour was given. The action not only rattled audibly (probably from 2³/₄-inch shells being shot in the 2¹/₂-inch chamber) but one barrel had a half-inch-long dent. Pieper was a big-time Belgian manufacturer of all grades of guns, and this was one of the cheaper. Despite all this Jay told me, "I'll just shoot light loads in it." I strongly advised him to put it on the wall and forget about it. I hope he has.

We have a pile of doubles in this house, but after my decades of searching I mostly use two. One is the Fox, with .008 inches of choke in the right barrel and .014 inches in the left. It is custom-stocked to fit me, and as a general-purpose shotgun for birds the size of pheasants or ducks, works perfectly. For lighter upland game I generally carry a Beretta Silver Hawk 16-gauge. This is not the Silver Hawk recently listed in their catalog, but an older gun. According to the proof marks it was made in 1957. It was built as an affordable double, so is far from fancy, but is nonetheless a really good gun. Made on a slightly smaller frame than most 12s, it has 70cm (27⁵/₈-inch) barrels and weighs a little over 6¹/₂ pounds, but is built to handle any commercial 16-gauge round, including Federal's excellent Premium 1¹/₄-ounce load. It had a pistol grip stock that I shot for a while, but eventually converted to straight grip. Unlike the present Silver Hawk, it has two trig-

Many hunters looking for a side-by-side buy a used gun. They're much cheaper than new models, with many bargains on the market right now.

88

gers, including that mark of a really good gun, an "articulated" front trigger, spring-hinged so that it won't bruise your finger during recoil.

Bill Heckman opened the very tight chokes to .005 inches and .015 inches, which has worked out perfectly. With 1-ounce loads using shot of average hard-

ness, it patterns perfectly for quail or ruffed grouse. With 1⅛-ounce loads it reaches just a bit farther for open-country birds like Hungarian and chukar partridge. With the heavy Federals the open barrel does fine on birds the size of sharp-tailed grouse or pheasants to 35 yards, and the tighter barrel produces genuine full-choke patterns.

The 16 is considered a weird choice these days, but you'll find more than a few when looking at used doubles, especially European guns, since until recently it was the most popular gauge over there. Even here the 16 held its own with the 20 until the 1960s, when the 3-inch 20 became popular as an all-around upland gun, using shells loaded with ⅞ to 1¼ ounces of shot. The story went that a "magnum" 20 could be used on everything from doves to ducks. All you had to do was buy the right shells. Since American-style 20s weigh about what the average British 12 weighs, around 6½ to 7 pounds, this sounded good. Most people bought the line, and many still do.

The problem with the theory is that the heavier loads for the 20 are a little too much for the small bore. Yes, they go bang, but operate at higher pressures than the equivalent 16- or 12-gauge loads, and at lower velocities. So the 3-inch 20 simply doesn't pattern as well as a 16. And since the loads are so much slower, it isn't easy to hit with, either. But the 16 still lost ground, especially after the advent of steel shot, since it couldn't hold a full ounce of steel.

Today the 16 remains the darling of a few serious uplands hunters. I started hunting in the mid-1960s, and was brainwashed early on by stories about the 3-inch 20, owning three or four. But this old Beretta works even better, especially on the larger upland birds we often encounter out here in the West. With bismuth shot, it cleanly takes the occasional mallard I jump while out after pheasants.

Both the Silver Hawk and the Fox cost less than $1,000, including the gunsmithing, and will last as long as I do. Since they both have simple extractors, the empties ride home in my game-vest pocket, rather than letting other hunters know where I find pheasants and ruffed grouse. If I someday write a best-seller there might be a drop-lock Westley Richards in the gun safe, the ultimate refinement of the boxlock, with only five moving parts in each removable lock. But for now I am content with my two old side-by-sides. A double gun implies simplicity, and the longer I live and hunt the more desirable simple seems to be.

The author about to drop an Alabama cockbird.

Most modern hunters prefer the over-under. Joe Coogan chose a 20-gauge Weatherby Orion for high-flying doves, because tight chokes could be screwed into both barrels. But the fixed-choked side-by-side still provides versatility when you don't know at what range a bird will appear.

Valley quail cover in southwestern Idaho.

A walk through the oaks in Mearns quail country, just north of the Mexican border.

93

CHAPTER FIVE

ALL-AMERICAN REPEATERS

The repeating shotgun reloads a single chamber quickly and repeatedly, hence its name. Repeaters are almost an entirely American invention, and not quite as new-fangled as some people believe. The first pump-action shotgun, the Spencer, was produced in the 1880s, in the same decade Winchester brought out its spectacularly ugly 1884 lever-action. In 1899 John Browning perfected the design of an autoloading shotgun, produced by the Browning company as the A-5 and by Remington as the Model 1911. This turn-of-the-century design turned out to be one of the most popular and long-lived shotguns of all time, only recently discontinued by Browning.

Pump and autoloader guns dominated the repeater market almost immediately. Winchester's lever gun only lasted a little past World War I. A few bolt-action shotguns are still manufactured, though these days most bolt shotguns are used for shooting slugs at deer, rather than flinging shot at flying birds. Lever and bolt-action shotguns take too long to "repeat" to allow practical follow-up shots on coveys of quail, or even single pheasants.

Right here I will explain why "pump" and "autoloader" have been and will be the words of choice to describe our two repeating shotguns. You may read that the pump is also called the "slide" or "trombone" action. Perhaps back in 1890 it was, but in decades of sitting in duck blinds and country cafes, I have never once heard a hunter talk about his slide-action shotgun, much less his faithful old trombone. So forget those terms.

"Autoloader" is a little more complicated. You'll hear them called automatics and semi-autos, but the first is technically incorrect (an automatic firearm is a "machine gun" that continues firing as long as the trigger is held back) while "semi-auto" not only seems imprecise, but these days has been so frequently and negatively used by the national media that it dredges up images of lunatic-fringe "militiamen" and inner-city gangs. So it won't be seen here.

Pumps and autoloaders have some advantages over double guns, and some disadvantages. On the plus side, even the most expensive autoloader is cheaper to manufacture than an equal-quality double. Serviceable pumps can be made to sell for $200, complete with screw-in chokes. While both are slightly more prone to malfunctions than good doubles, the pump is almost as reliable, even with ratty old reloads. And modern autoloaders work nearly as reliably, though more care must be taken when constructing handloads. For practical wingshooting either can be fired as fast as a double, if not faster, with more shots in reserve. Contrary to the belief of many double snobs, more than two shots can be a definite advantage in some kinds of bird hunting. And sometimes—dare I say it?—three shots can be more ethical, since the third shot can finish off a cripple that might escape a double-gunner trying to fumble more shells into the chambers.

On the negative side, repeaters usually don't balance quite as nicely as doubles, though balance really depends on the individual gun. I've shot many doubles that felt like checkered 2x4's, and a few pumps and autoloaders that rivaled the finest London game gun. Sadly, finely balanced pumps seem to be almost a thing of the past. They used to be made with smaller receivers for smaller gauges, and most didn't feature ventilated ribs, so before 1960 it was fairly easy to buy a very light, nice-handling pumpgun in about any gauge. A classic example was the original Winchester Model 12, chambered in 20-gauge with a 25-inch barrel. Soon other gauges followed, including heavier-framed duck guns, but it was the 6-pound 20 that convinced many shooters to try a pump.

These days the Model 12 has been brought back in various limited-run reproductions. The last model I can find in the catalogs is also a 20-gauge, but with a blocky Monte Carlo stock and heavy ventilated-rib barrel, weighing more than 7 pounds. I mean, why bother? Today most light pumps are made light by

The repeater has been a choice of American hunters since the turn of the century. Here Mike Jordan shoots an old Winchester Model 97 on a Mississippi duck hunt.

chopping off several inches of barrel. This doesn't affect their handling as adversely as it does in short-barreled doubles, since the machinery in a pump's forend keeps some weight forward. But for most upland hunting, I still prefer one of the older guns, with a small frame and longer, unribbed barrel.

A slim, light pump like one of Winchester's old Model 12s has gained the admiration of some elite double-gunners. Gough Thomas even invented a word to describe the pump's operation. He called them "eumatic," which meant that pumps naturally lend themselves to the human body's own mechanics. Even to an Englishman like Thomas, the opening of the action with the forend hand during recoil seemed entirely natural, while the forward reloading motion brings a pumpgun back into alignment on a flying bird.

It does take some strength and coordination to really run a pump, but to those who've done it for a long time the gun almost seems to work itself. And I agree with Thomas's evaluation of the pump's natural "repointing" ability. When time allows I tend to work the forend at a fairly leisurely pace, allowing the forward stroke to bring the shotgun smoothly in front of a flying mallard. But if the shooting needs to be quick, I can make a pumpgun go bang just as fast as a two-trigger double gun, and have used pumps to kill two ruffed grouse that flushed together. Many pumpgunners are even faster.

Two basic mechanical methods run autoloaders: recoil and gas. Recoil-operated guns feature a spring-loaded barrel that, upon firing, slides backward inside the action pushing the empty shell against a fixed ejector. It then picks up a fresh round on its way back. While fairly reliable, the recoil system tends to accentuate the shotgun's kick or, at the very least, does nothing to relieve it. For many years most autoloaders were fairly heavy, and thought of primarily as duck guns or big-country pheasant guns, useful only for long-range shooting. There were exceptions, such as Browning's Sweet 16 A-5, and Franchi's marvelous little lightweights. But they were still exceptions, not the rule.

The gas gun started to change all that. Essentially, these are pump guns operated by a gas cylinder rather than the shooter's hand. In a pump, a couple of rods link the forend with the bolt of the action. When the shooter pulls the forend back, the action opens; when the forend is shoved forward, the action closes. In a gas autoloader the rods are linked to a piston inside the forend. Gas from the burning powder is "bled" (leaked) through a tiny hole inside the barrel, which pushes the piston backwards and opens the bolt. A heavy spring pushes the bolt forward again.

Sears, Roebuck and Co. marketed the first gas guns in the 1950s. Early on they had a reputation for two things: lighter kick and poor reliability. The recoil isn't really lighter in a gas gun, it's just spread out over a few more milliseconds, but the softening effect was definitely there from the beginning. Consequently gas guns have become favored for any type of wingshooting involving hard recoil or repeated shots. Lots of duck and goose hunters have switched to gas guns, which really take the sting out of 12- and 10-gauge magnums. Many dove hunters also like gas autoloaders, especially if they travel outside the United States to Mexico or South America where limits (if they exist at all) are much higher than the 10 or 15 birds a day common up here. And even if the stateside limit is 15 birds a day, many shooters need 40 or 50 shots to collect their 15 doves. That can add up over a morning.

Of course, some shooters are just plain recoil sensitive, and it's not necessarily just kids or women, as many macho hunters assume. The worst flincher I've ever seen was my friend Kirby Matthew, who grew up in the tiny town of Trout Creek in extreme western Montana. Kirby started shooting a .300 magnum at elk when he was 14 years old, because he'd hit one badly with a lighter rifle and decided he needed more power. He soon developed the mother of all flinches. There isn't much bird shooting in the thick trees around Trout Creek either, so Kirby didn't get much practice with a scatter-gun. When he did move somewhere he could hunt birds, Kirby started missing. His solution? The shotgun equivalent of the .300 magnum: more powder and more shot. I once sat in a duck blind over a pothole with Kirby and in two hours collected a limit with my 20-gauge. Kirby had two birds by then, and had to run to town to buy another box of magnum 12s. Since then he has learned the virtues of lighter recoil and better shooting, but a lot of macho men haven't.

The reliability of autoloaders has only recently been truly improved. Twenty years ago I wouldn't have used an autoloader for any kind of hunting, especially not a gas gun for ducks in cold Montana Novembers, because they jammed too damn often and had to be cleaned constantly. But those days are just about gone.

Though repeaters supposedly don't balance as well as doubles, there are many exceptions. This little Franchi 20-gauge weighs 5-1/2 pounds and balances better than many super-light doubles, as evidenced by the pair of Arizona Gambel's quail.

Many shooters pick gas-operated autoloaders for waterfowling because of their softer felt recoil.

In the past couple of years I've used both Beretta and Browning gas-operated autoloaders to shoot several hundred rounds without cleaning, in all sorts of weather, without a single malfunction.

Despite that, many hunters still pick recoil-operated guns for really tough use. Benelli's autoloader has a great reputation among waterfowlers. One of my Southern duck-hunting friends, Claude Bannister, recently told a story about walking out to a pit blind early one morning with a couple of buddies, one of whom was rather large and ungainly. He fell into the blind, which had several inches of water and mud in the bottom, and couldn't get up. Claude and his other friend had to lift the big man out to solve the problem. They grabbed anything they could, and somehow found some hard handles underneath their muddy buddy's camo parka. The handles turned out to be Claude's Benelli, which despite being pounded into the mud, functioned perfectly after a quick rinse in murky water. That's about as tough as a gun can get;

20 years ago I'd have bet that only a pumpgun could take such punishment.

One of any autoloader's disadvantages used to be an inability to use shells of different lengths and strengths, while doubles and pumps can load and eject anything from short, light-kicking target loads to long, heavy-hitting magnums. Recoil operated guns attempt to get around this by using a friction ring on the forend tube. This can be turned around to allow the barrel to jerk back at different speeds. It works, at least some of the time.

In the past couple of years there have been several versatile gas autoloaders marketed, most notably the Browning Gold. I have mentioned this gun several times already, simply because it seems about as close to perfection as an all-around autoloader can get. Mine has fired everything from target loads to $3^1/_2$-inch magnums without any adjustment whatsoever and, at a little over $7^1/_2$ pounds, works equally well on sporting clays, late-season pheasants or long-range Canada geese. Besides taking the sting out of what are essentially 10-gauge loads, it has an interrupted sear mechanism, and is one of the most easily field-stripped shotguns of any type I've ever used. Winchester offers the same gun as the X2, minus a couple of frills. I recently used a new short-barreled camouflage version of the Gold, weighing only 7¼ pounds, to hunt both bobwhite quail and wild turkeys in Alabama. It worked equally well on both.

Prior to the last few years, the only autoloader I'd owned was a 5½-pound Franchi 20-gauge, a marvelous little gun, just as slim and well-balanced as any fine double, with a straight grip, a little cast-off and a clean, 3½-pound trigger pull. But these days my Browning Gold takes the place of my old Remington 870 pumpgun on many hunts.

So today's autoloaders are better than ever, while the pumps have slipped backward. There's nothing wrong with Remington's 870 or Browning's BPS or Winchester's 1300, but despite all the options—synthetic stocks, barrel lengths, screw-in chokes—the real options are rather limited. Sure you can buy just about any sort of 3-inch 12-gauge you want (or even a 3½-inch 12- or 10-gauge), and it'll work fine for anything you want a heavy 12-gauge to do.

But because they're built on 12-gauge frames, many pump 20s are too heavy. The best for upland shooting are the various short-barreled, straight-gripped models usually known, aptly enough, as upland or field models. Most come in around 6½ pounds or a little more, and work pretty well as upland guns, though I sure wish they'd make them in 16-gauge. If you're not fairly strong, however, a straight-grip pump is harder to hold onto while you're running the forend back and forth. I made the mistake of buying exactly such a gun for my wife's first shotgun. Eileen never could shuck it quickly, and consequently now much prefers doubles and autoloaders.

While the 20-gauge upland guns are light enough, most pump 28s and .410s are way too heavy. I recently

While pumpguns work fine in the uplands, many modern pumps are too heavy. This Montana sharp-tailed grouse hunter carries an old Ithaca Model 37 Featherweight, a classic upland pump.

tried copies of Remington's .410 870 and Browning's 28-gauge BPS. The Remington only comes in their cheap Express model, with a "walnut-stained hardwood stock" and a fixed full choke. Because it's built on exactly the same frame as their 12-gauge magnums, it weighs 6$\frac{1}{2}$ pounds. The BPS 28 was a higher-grade gun, with screw-in chokes, but even heavier at 7$\frac{1}{4}$ pounds.

Yeah, I know why this is happening: The pump has become the bottom-line choice among bird hunters, something cheap to start with until you can afford a good autoloader or double. But it breaks my heart. Mossberg does make a nifty little 22-inch-barreled 20-gauge called the Bantam that only weighs about six pounds, but the best all-around pump I've seen lately is the re-born Ithaca Model 37, which now comes in (cries of joy!) 16-gauge, as well as 20 and 12.

But if you really want a good upland pumpgun (and in later chapters I'll tell exactly why you might) don't forget the used market. Since these days many pumps get traded for autoloaders or doubles, there are a bunch of them out there. My friend Jay Rightnour just bought a beautiful little Remington 870 28-gauge lightweight weighing 6 pounds, with two barrels choked skeet and modified, for $350. Made with a mahogany stock, this model was very nicely finished and balanced—and compare its weight to the Remington .410 and Browning 28 mentioned above. There are others: old 20-gauge Ithaca 37's weighing 5$\frac{1}{2}$ pounds, ribless Remington Wingmasters from the 1950s, or Model 12 Winchesters in 16-gauge. (These have now become fairly hot items—to be converted to 28-gauge, since original Model 12 in 28 costs several thousand dollars. Just why

These days the pumpgun is looked on as an inexpensive, rugged repeater for hard duty. This duck hunter shoots a synthetic-stocked Remington 870, about as tough a gun as you can buy.

most wingshooters would want a 28 instead of a 16 eludes me, but there it is.) You might even run into a Remington Model 31, the "ball-bearing shotgun," that had the reputation of being perhaps the slickest-working ever, but couldn't compete during the Great Depression with Winchester's established Model 12.

The one disadvantage of older pumpguns is fixed chokes, but this is no real disadvantage. If you're really finicky, have screw-in chokes installed, but if they're improved cylinder or modified, I'd leave them be. Then select ammo to cover the ranges. The modified barrel of my old Winchester Model 12 in 16-gauge actually has .010 inches of constriction, somewhere between modern improved cylinder and modified. With 1-ounce "cheap" loads of #7$\frac{1}{2}$ it works fine on smaller close-range birds at 20 to 30 yards. With Federal's 1$\frac{1}{4}$-ounce Premium magnums it throws nearly full choke patterns, and has killed a number of pheasants at 40 yards.

The single choke is also supposed to be something of a disadvantage when compared to the two chokes of a double. For some kinds of shooting it is, but when every shot comes at long range, the single barrel is an advan-

Several modern repeaters have reversible safeties to accommodate left-handed shooters.

Sharp-tailed grouse flushing from brushy draw.

tage. The typical fixed-choke, classic side-by-side is not the best gun to use on long-range birds, because its open barrel will only wound at more than 35 yards. So you'll essentially be shooting a one-shot gun. A repeater choked modified or full is a much better choice.

I admit to being something of a pump-nut (as if you couldn't tell by now), my oldest self-indulgence being my outside-hammer Model 97 Winchester, stocked in extra-fancy black walnut, re-blued and fitted with screw-in chokes. At $7^3/_4$ pounds it's really too heavy to carry across the pheasant hills, though I generally take it after sage grouse every year or two, which often means even more walking. But it's one of two or three guns I reach for when a duck dinner is in order. With an improved-modified choke tube and a magazine full of bismuth 4's, it will cleanly kill mallards at 50 yards, but also points so precisely that I can head-shoot decoying birds at 15 yards.

I grew up with side-by-sides, never firing a pumpgun at game until I was 20, and it was the same old 97 that did the trick. It belonged to Ben Burshia, my first wife's grandfather, one of those highly practical old-time Montana hunters who owned a 12-gauge shotgun, a .30-06 and a .22—and handily killed every kind of game in the state with those three guns. By the time I hunted with him, Ben was 75 years old, and I never saw him miss a sharp-tail, Hun, pheasant or duck in two autumns.

The first time I used the 97 was on sharp-tailed grouse. Ben knew the location of a big chokecherry patch, and even in early September birds of all kinds flock to the last drying chokecherries. We parked the pickup a quarter-mile away, and he sent me in with the 97 and his Labrador/Heinz-57 hunting dog Susie. I had never fired a pump before, but had used several lever-action Marlin and Winchester rifles. This old hammer-pump appeared to be exactly the same gun, just operated by a pump instead of a lever.

The first sharptail got up 30 yards away and the long-barreled shotgun seemed to take forever to come to my shoulder. But when I touched the crisp trigger the bird went down. This happened three more times, and then a final bird got up on the far side of the cherry patch. I wasn't going to even try, but Ben hollered "Shoot!" and the old gun did, seemingly somewhere outside my will. And the grouse fell, so far away that I couldn't believe it. Ben told me it was a trained gun. He must have shot several thousand birds with it over his lifetime.

That happens with a lot of people, once they actually start shooting pumps and autoloaders. Part of it, I believe, is the machinery in the forend, which tends to smooth out the swing. But part of it is the single sighting plane, and the crisp triggers of many pumps and even some autoloaders. Good older guns tend to have better triggers than those coming out of the factories these days, though most modern triggers are easily fixed. It only took 30 minutes to change my Gold's trigger from a creepy 6-pounder to a crisp 3³/₄-pound pull, and a good gunsmith doesn't take much longer to fix an 870.

But back when shotguns used to be made out of milled steel instead of stampings and aluminum, trigger mechanisms stayed in adjustment much longer—and so could be made crisper and lighter in the first place. When Ben Burshia decided to sell me his old 97 (because it had grown too heavy for a 77-year-old man), I measured the trigger pull at 3¹/₂ pounds. And that's exactly what it measures today, more than 20 years later.

Judy Cornell and her Beretta, wondering just where the pheasants are.

A mallard set in flooded timber.

Today's pumps, quickly turned out on computer-controlled machinery, do not offer the same precision, though you can purchase aftermarket trigger assemblies for popular models.

The triggers of modern autoloaders seem to be somewhat better than modern pumps, especially those of Italian guns. In fact, autoloaders seem to be receiving the production attention that pumps used to get, mostly because people are willing to spend more money on them. It seems nobody will pay much more than $300 for a pump these days, while many popular autoloaders run closer to $1,000. At those prices you can expect better triggers, finer wood, better finishing and more polished mechanics.

As autoloaders have grown more reliable, more hunters trust them, so they're made in a much wider variety than they used to be, something like the variety we used to see in pumpguns. I have already mentioned the super-light little Franchi 20-gauge, just about as perfect a light upland gun as I've ever shot. It also comes in 12- and 28-gauge, and I just may have to own one of the 28s someday. The advertised weight of the 20 is 5.2 pounds, but mine weighs almost exactly $5\frac{1}{2}$. So what? Five-and-a-half is light enough for any shotgunning, and at that weight it balances and swings better than all but the finest small-gauge doubles.

Other companies make very good upland autoloaders. Beretta's AL390 Silver Mallard in 20-gauge weighs a little under $6\frac{1}{2}$ pounds, and Weatherby just started importing a similar 20 made, I believe, in Japan. Remington makes their fine little 11-87, which in its 23-inch-barreled, straight-gripped Special Field version weighs 6½ pounds. All these guns work much better on most smaller upland birds than the typical "duck and pheasant" autoloader.

One frequent complaint about repeaters is their awkward safeties. I especially hear this from double-gunners used to the logical, eumatic tang safety, right there on the top of the grip, and equally handy for right- and left-handers. Most pumps and autoloaders have safeties at the front or rear of the triggerguard, a crossbolt that must be pushed sideways. Most of today's guns have the safety at the rear of the guard, but Model 12 Winchesters had it in front. This can take some getting used to, especially for someone who's long shot an 870 Remington, with its rear safety. I use both and have found that resting my trigger finger outside the front or rear of the triggerguard, depending on the safety's location, works for me. But if you're really addicted to the tang safety, Browning's BPS pumpgun features exactly that, and the Mossberg 500 has the safety at the top rear of the receiver.

Left-handers often find triggerguard safeties awkward, since they must reach around to the other side of the guard to punch the safety off. Buying a BPS or a Mossberg is one solution, but several of the newer repeaters feature reversible safeties. There is also the ultimate solution, which doesn't work for most hunters. My friend Liz Lewis, for several years one of the top sporting clays shooters, once had the safety of her Beretta jam at an inopportune time during a match. So she took her pliers and jerked the thing completely out of there, leaving a slightly ragged hole in the triggerguard. This is obviously no handicap for target shooting, but it might be awkward to hunt with an empty chamber, jacking in a round when a pheasant rises.

Pumps and autoloaders are also the easiest guns to fit. As mentioned earlier, the buttstocks on most repeaters are held on by a through-bolt, and the head of the stock can be rasped to change drop or cast. But several repeaters feature adjustable stocks. This isn't an exactly new idea—the century-old Winchester 97's stock was somewhat adjustable—but it's still a good one.

Thanksgiving dinner on your back.

A rooster pheasant, a pumpgun and a Labrador retriever: a common scene on the American hunting landscape.

CHAPTER SIX

PHEASANTS

About a decade ago an article appeared in a hunting magazine about a pheasant hunter who, after shooting thousands of birds, had decided that a Browning Superposed 20-gauge with 3-inch chambers, shooting #7½ shot, was the perfect pheasant gun. At the time I had not shot thousands of pheasants (and still haven't) but had killed a few hundred in my years of pursuing roosters in eastern Montana and the Dakotas. Many fell to at least three 20-gauge magnums, and for a couple of years I'd experimented with 7½'s.

But after a few years I started leaving my 20s at home after pheasant season opened. The Montana pheasant opener is five weeks after the state's other

On point in southwestern Idaho. It could be a Hun, chukar partridge, valley quail, pheasant, sharp-tail or sage grouse. You won't know until it's in the air.

Pheasants are the most popular upland bird in North America.

Wild pheasants typically flush at longer range than preserve birds and are much tougher to kill cleanly.

upland seasons begins. I carried the 20s earlier in the fall for Hungarian partridge and ruffed grouse hunts. Even with 3-inch shells, the 20 simply did not work as well as a 12-gauge on pheasant. At the time of this article I hadn't shot at a pheasant in 15 years with 7½'s, having plucked too many pellets from the butt-end of birds that took more than one shot—or a long Labrador chase—to bring to hand.

So I read on, intrigued with why someone with so much experience should choose such a wimpy shotgun. After all, maybe I was just a bad shot. But it turned out this expert had killed almost all his birds at a shooting preserve in the Midwest. Aha! I said, and threw the magazine across the room.

As somebody wise once pointed out, experience can be deep but narrow. Many bird hunters I run into make the same blanket statement that pheasants are too easy to hit, and a few have even claimed that a 28-gauge is a totally adequate rooster gun. But as we talk, it eventually grows plain that every one of those

shooters has "hunted" mostly on game preserves.

I have nothing against shooting pen-raised pheasants, having done it quite a few times myself, usually at the invitation of shotgun and ammunition manufacturers wanting me to test their wares. Preserve pheasants can provide a lot of shooting in a few short hours, which gives an experienced hunter some idea of how a gun or load works. They also provide hunting of a sort near the suburban sprawl that chews up more and more real hunting country every year, and good basic training for young dogs and shooters.

But preserve hunting doesn't tell much about how a gun and load works on wild pheasants in a cornfield, and most especially not on 2-year-old roosters. There are several reasons for this. First, pen-raised birds get thrown into the cold cruel world when quite young. This is an economic necessity: The longer pheasants live in pens, the more each bird costs in food and labor. So a profitable shooting preserve must push birds out of the nest, so to speak, as soon as they can fly.

As a result, many preserve roosters have barely changed color from the hen-brown of youth. Many have dull feathers mixed with the bright green of their heads, and tails barely longer than their bodies. Such young birds also have thinner skin than old birds, and not nearly as many feathers as a wild bird ready to endure a South Dakota winter.

Such innocent young pheasants also tend to hold very tightly. I once walked around a bush on a preserve to find a recently released rooster sitting on the ground 10 feet away. He looked up at me oddly, as if wondering when I'd throw out some grain. I took a step closer. He still looked at me. I walked up and gently toed him in the tailfeathers, and if roosters had butt-cheeks he'd have clenched them. After a few more seconds he decided he might fly away. I waited patiently for him to rise 15 yards, then whacked him with the cylinder barrel of my AyA. Combine young bodies, lack of feathers and close holding, and you can indeed kill such birds with small shot, and not much

of it.

Here I must also mention driven birds. It's often pointed out by light-load advocates that driven pheasants in the British Isles and Europe are typically killed by open-choked shotguns throwing an ounce of shot, or maybe slightly more. This is true. It is also true that 99 percent of the driven pheasants shot these days are pen-raised, and most are killed flying toward the gun, or overhead. The shot must only penetrate the tender breast meat and maybe a rib before reaching the vitals.

But wild pheasant seasons don't open until young roosters have grown reasonably long tails. Here in Montana we have a fairly early mid-October opening date, but many states don't allow pheasants to be chased until November. These are 6-month-old birds, rather than the 4-month-old birds shot on preserves. By late fall the skin of wild birds is much tougher, and the feathers almost as thick as sheep's wool. Throw in a few of last year's birds (which after a mild winter can amount to a third of wild roosters) and pheasant

High pheasant cover in North Dakota.

killing can get very tough. Try driving an ounce of small shot through the pelvis of a 45-yard December rooster with an open-choked shotgun, and you'll only speed him up.

The story of my all-time toughest pheasant involves my old friend Norm Strung, who hunted as my guest on a northeastern Montana riverbottom. Norm carried a 12-gauge pump, while I had my Stevens 20-gauge magnum side-by-side. We posted one end of a long buffalo-berry patch, while our two partners started with a pair of black Labradors from the other end.

Soon a rooster got up in front of the dogs. One friend shot and missed, but the bird flew toward Norm and me, as we stood 35 yards apart on either side of the brush. As the pheasant flew closer Norm raised his gun and shot, knocking off quite a few feathers. But the bird didn't fall, so I shot, hitting it solidly almost directly overhead. Norm's second shot hit the bird immediately afterward, but the pheasant kept flying, so I gave it my tight barrel going away. All four shots had

hit the bird, at least three very solidly, yet it kept on flapping, though by now losing altitude like an Alaskan float plane with a badly sputtering engine. It was still flapping when it hit the ground nearly 100 yards away. By the time one of the Labs ran over there and picked it up, the pheasant was quite dead. Norm said it must have sunk from the sheer weight of #6 shot, and broken its neck on impact.

So there are pheasant guns, and then there are pheasant guns. When working on an eastern Montana ranch as a teenager, the rancher's same-age son used a side-by-side .410. Ralph killed quite a few roosters with that little gun, but he was one of the finest instinctive shots I've ever seen, and rattlesnake quick. Still, the few birds he shot at over 25 yards tended to fly away, still cackling.

I've never used the .410 on pheasants, but have cleanly killed many preserve birds with the 28 and #7½ and #6 shot, the 6's coming mostly from Winchester's 1-ounce load. This heavy 28 load is derided by purists, who insist that ¾ of an ounce is all a 28 can

Cattail draw, central Montana.

handle "perfectly." But in every 28 I've ever tried it in, Winchester's little "magnum" patterns "perfectly." One entire fall I hunted as many different upland birds as I could with the 28, from quail to sage grouse, and noticed that when the birds got bigger, an ounce of 6's worked far better than ³/₄-ounce of anything. Yeah, the 1-ounce load starts a little slower, but you shouldn't be shooting any bird further than 35 yards with a 28 anyway. Closer than that, and you'll hardly notice the velocity loss. Even then, I would no more hunt wild pheasants with a 28 than take a 20 after Canada geese. By picking and choosing your shots, you could certainly kill a few roosters or geese, but my wild pheasant and goose hunting is tough enough with having to limit shots to 35 yards.

The problem with the 28-gauge, despite its short shot string and even patterns, is it shoots at most an ounce of shot. After due deliberation over hundreds of wild roosters, I will flatly state that an ounce of shot is not enough for all-around shooting of wild pheasants, particularly after the first week of the season. By then the young, dumb birds have been killed and the survivors are even more wild. Shots will be longer at tougher birds.

So how much shot is enough? Let me introduce here the concept of pattern density versus bird size. The 30-inch circle at 40 yards has long been the standard for percentage patterning. As mentioned in the ammunition chapter, an improved cylinder choke supposedly puts about half its shot in a 30-inch circle at 40 yards, a modified choke about 60 percent, and full choke 70 percent.

It might seem that the 30-inch circle is arbitrary, but in the field a 30-inch circle encompasses a very useful shot-spread, providing the average shooter some leeway for error. An average full choke will put virtually all its shot in a 30-inch circle at 25 yards, and that's about as close as you want to shoot birds with full. Any closer and you'll either miss, because the pattern's so small, or the bird will best be served as pheasant-burger.

It was also mentioned in the ammunition chapter

A new Labrador bouncing through the pheasant grass.

that wingshooters generally agree that unless at least four pellets hit a medium-sized gamebird, odds are none will strike a vital area. On a tough bird like a pheasant, five hits are none too few.

The body of a mature pheasant, flying directly away, forms a circle about 5 inches in diameter. The area of this circle (remember your junior-high math, now) can be figured by squaring the radius of five (2.5 inches) then multiplying by pi (3.142). The result is 19.64 square inches. Let's make things easy and call it 20.

Now let's figure out the pattern density of an ounce of #6 shot through a full choke barrel. (We're using 6's because anything smaller won't penetrate a going-away pheasant at 40 yards. This has been determined by millions of field experiments over the years, performed by volunteers in Nebraska, Kansas, Iowa and the Dakotas.) A 30-inch circle's area can be found by the same formula: $15 \times 15 \times 3.142 = 706.95$. Again, let's make things simple and call it 700 square inches.

With those numbers, we can find the density of a full choke, 1-ounce load of 6's at 40 yards. According to the tables from ammunition makers, there are about 225 #6 lead pellets in an ounce. Since 70 percent of them will land in our circle, .70 times 225 equals about 160 shot.

Dividing the 700 square inches of our 30-inch circle by 160, we find an average of one #6 shot in each 4.4 square inches. That's an average; shotgun patterns tend to be clumpy. Sparce in some places, more dense in others. But all shotgunning involves playing the odds.

Now we divide the 20-inch body-area of a retreating pheasant by 4.4. This indicates that with a 1-ounce load out of a full choke, about 4.5 #6 shot strikes the rooster's body at 40 yards.

That's, of course, an average. Most of the time, either four or five pellets will hit our pheasant. This implies a clean kill. Or does it? Remember, we made these calculations with a full choke gun. Most of us hit far better with the wider spread of modified, or even improved cylinder, especially at closer ranges. With full choke we'll miss some closer birds, or turn them into McPheasant patties.

Working the same numbers with modified (60 percent) results in 3.85 hits at 40 yards, while improved cylinder (50 percent) works out to 3.2 hits. Some of

the time these will result in clean kills, but more often you'll have to chase down lively birds. Without a good dog you'll lose a few. Hell, even with a good dog you'll lose some. Yes, you can kill pheasants dead in the air with less than 1¼ ounces of shot, but you'd better hold your fire past 30 or 35 yards, depending on the shot and load.

The wild pheasants that get up in front of my Labs over the average season rise at any range from boot-toe to 40 yards or more. Both human and dogs work pretty hard to get those shots, either in sore feet or finding a place to hunt, and I don't like to pass up any reasonable shot just because I'm undergunned. Over the years I have also noticed that many people shoot at any rooster they think might fall, whether they're carrying a 28-gauge or a 12-gauge magnum.

In the thick riverbottoms where I find a lot of wild pheasants these days, once the birds reach 30 yards they're often gone behind an alder or cottonwood. So improved cylinder is a good choice. But the roosters that rise farther out are better handled by modified. About .010 inches of choke from a 20, 16 or 12 will do the trick, and .015 inches will provide 65 to 70 percent patterns with premium loads in most guns.

Since most shots are at single roosters, my favorite pheasant gun is double-choked; the classic improved cylinder and modified, using 1¼ ounces of hard #6 shot. In the days when I could afford only handloads filled with the cheapest shot, I liked 5's, but hard 6's penetrate just as well (if not better) even at 45 yards, with more pattern density. The 3-inch 20-gauge will work, but 20s rarely pattern as well as 16s or 12s, even with extra-hard buffered shot, and the slow muzzle velocity of the 1¼-ounce loads make hitting tougher past 25 yards. So a 12-gauge (or a 16 if you have one) provides a small but definite edge.

My top all-around pheasant gun is my old Fox Sterlingworth. Weighing exactly 7 pounds, it's light enough to carry all day, but heavy enough to swing well on 40-yard shots, and can withstand the pounding of 1¼-ounce loads. It patterns Winchester's Super Pigeon load of hard copper-plated 6's superbly. With a muzzle velocity of 1,220 fps this isn't a super-fast round, but a hard-hitting load for live-pigeon shooting, when the pigeon needs to be stopped, not just hit. In a light field gun it kicks noticeably less than faster shells, and works great as a general purpose pheasant load. The improved cylinder barrel provides pheasant patterns to 35 yards, while the modified barrel has cleanly dropped roosters out to 45.

Neither Federal nor Remington offers #6 shot in their pigeon loads which, because of the big money in pigeon shooting, tend to be among the finest shot-

The author's favorite general-purpose pheasant gun is his 12-gauge Fox Sterlingworth, made in 1905. A two-trigger double provides an instant choice of chokes, whether the rooster rises at your feet or 40 yards.

Both repeaters and doubles work for late-season pheasant shooting, but they should be equipped with at least a modified choke.

shells in any manufacturer's line. But Federal's Premium High-Brass copper-plated load patterns almost as well, though at 1,330 fps it kicks harder in light guns. It makes a fine long-range load when you need it, though. Remington, unfortunately, doesn't offer a similar load of plated shot. Their 1¼-ounce 12-gauge loads are either their Express (1,330 fps), using hard but unplated shot, or their 1,220 fps Heavy Field load, with softer shot. Their only copper-plated 12 loads are heavy-kicking magnums using at least 1½ ounces of shot. A few pheasant hunters also swear by Fiocchi's nickel-plated loads, which penetrate very well indeed. I definitely recommend hard, plated shot for wild roosters. It patterns and penetrates better than unplated shot, no matter how hard.

If hunting lowlands where mallards might be jumped, common in the heart of wild pheasant coun-

try, the Bismuth Upland Game load with 6's provides exactly the same ballistics as Winchester's Pigeon load, and performance on birds seems almost identical. Before bismuth I tried steel when hunting along streams, but never found a load that would both penetrate and provide the pattern density needed for 40-yard pheasants. Plus, I hated biting steel when eating both pheasants *and* ducks.

A light 12-gauge over-under is also a fine choice for all-around pheasant shooting, it's only disadvantage is a lack of instant choke choice. A pumpgun or autoloader choked modified works too, but most 12s are too damned heavy to carry all day—unless you require a real late-season prairie cannon. December and January birds turn very wild, and some days no shot seems to come at less than 40 yards. Here a 3-inch 12-gauge works best, and even a 3½-inch gun might not be out of line, since at more than 45 yards #5 and even #4 shot penetrates better on thick-skinned winter roosters. You'll need at least 1¹/₂ ounces and full choke to consistently drop such long-range birds. There's no need for two chokes, so fixed-choke doubles aren't ideal, though a tight modified and full will work. Better yet is an over-under equipped with screw-in chokes, with two full tubes in place, or a full-choked pump or autoloader.

Another rather specialized pheasant gun can come in handy, depending on how much you like to suffer in the field. When hunting pressure turns heavy, a lot of wild roosters move into cattail and alder swamps. This hunting requires hip boots or even chest waders, but under the right (wrong?) conditions the birds are definitely there. This closely resembles ruffed grouse

shooting, but with tougher birds. Ranges tend toward very close, so the 20-gauge works about as well as the 12, though I still prefer at least 1¹/₈ ounces of shot, and a lighter gun is a definite advantage. I've used a number of doubles for this work, including a 20-gauge magnum Stevens side-by-side, a 25-inch barreled AyA 12, and my present favorite, a 6¹/₂-pound Beretta. But any open-choked, fairly short and light gun of 20-gauge or more will do the job.

Wild pheasants are glorious birds to hunt, to gaze upon, and eat. By all accounts they're the most popular upland bird in America, despite being transplanted foreigners—but then again, so are all of us, including the First Americans who live mostly on reservations. With the exception of a big sage grouse, they're also the toughest upland bird on the continent, and by far

Late-season pheasant hunting, northern Wyoming.

Under heavy hunting pressure many pheasants hide in thick cover, where a light, open-choked double works better than anything else.

An ounce of shot is not enough for all-around hunting of wild pheasants. Bill Gallea shoots a 20-gauge, but almost exclusively with 3-inch magnum shells.

the hardest to catch when wounded. While dainty little 28s and 20s are fine for preserve birds, or early-season roosters hunted over good pointing dogs, for all-around shooting of wild pheasants I must depend on the wisdom of novelist and African hunter Robert Ruark, who put it quite plainly: "Use enough gun." A prairie rooster that's survived a Dakota winter, coming out of the cattails with tailfeathers streaming behind him like the banner of independence, deserves a clean death.

Lunch during a pheasant hunt.

Late afternoon along
pheasant cover.

Few birds match the
majesty of a rooster
pheasant.

123

CHAPTER SEVEN

QUAILS AND DOVES

Thirty years ago most hunters automatically thought "bobwhite" when anybody mentioned quail, but today the idea that quail come in other shapes, and live in other places than the Southeast, has slowly entered the wingshooter's collective consciousness. Quail live not just all across the United States, but as far north as British Columbia, and the best wild bobwhite quail hunting today is found in the midsection of the country, far from the Georgia pines, from Texas up through Nebraska and Iowa.

These days, most of the "traditional" Southern

To many hunters "quail" always means bobwhite. Eileen Clarke points her 16-gauge at a quail on White Oak Plantation in Alabama.

quail hunting involves pen-raised birds. The truly good wild-quail hunting anywhere south of the Mason-Dixon Line and east of Texas requires land managed for quail, and hardly anything else. I know one wealthy Georgia plantation owner who, when one of his bird-hunting guests suggested that he was lucky to have such good quail hunting right there on his home place, said: "Lucky, hell! Each of those birds you shot this morning cost me $5,000."

So bobwhite quail in the South will cost you, either in money or social climbing—or boot leather. It is still possible to find a few coveys of wild quail, but the small farms that created such perfect bobwhite habitat during the share-cropping era have all but disappeared. A few very rich landowners can recreate their affect, but most of the small farms of the Old South have now turned into rows of planted pines or vast soybean fields. These make for pretty good deer hunting, but don't leave much room for bobwhite quail.

Despite all that, across a vast segment of the country when you say "bird hunting" people assume the bird is the bobwhite, and the traditions die hard. I have hunted southern quail, both wild and pen-raised, on foot and while sitting on the well-upholstered seat of a mule-drawn wagon, while a dog-handler rode ahead on a Tennessee Walker and a pair of bony pointers ranged across Alabama, and a black driver clucked at his matched pair of mules. The latter may not be "real" quail hunting to some people, but it's the closest most of us will ever get to the rhythms of the Old South. (Of course there are those who say the Old South wasn't such a good thing, but having spent plenty of time in the rural south, versus the urban south and north, I would suggest that the "new" rural south is a much better place for an outdoor person of any type than anyplace else east of the Mississippi River except, perhaps, the beautiful mountains and valleys of West Virginia.)

But it doesn't really matter to the quail hunter where in the traditional South bobwhites are hunted.

Southern quail country.

A traditional mule-drawn quail hunt in the deep South.

The gun and load are basically the same: a light shotgun shooting an ounce or even less of #7½ shot. Most shots at Southern quail come at 15 to 25 yards, and within that range even a .410 can do good work on bobwhites. As for choke, well, you might expect wide-open to be the rule, but it ain't necessarily so.

I know one exclusive wild-quail plantation that very much frowns on anybody shooting any gauge over 28. Their reasoning? Any bigger gauge causes too many inadvertent cripples, birds that aren't actually shot at on a covey rise, but are still hit by a pellet or two on the edge of the pattern. Since a wild Southern quail can cost several thousand dollars, not crippling any birds inadvertently makes sense. But why would the .410 and 28 cripple fewer than a 20- or 16-gauge?

Because of the chokes. Most .410s are choked tightly; there isn't much shot, so it needs to be concentrated. Twenty-eights vary more, but even traditional doubles tend to be choked modified and full, and many 28 fans (including me) favor those chokes, just to get the most out of the little gauge.

But bigger gauges (and on bobwhites a 20 is a bigger gauge) have enough pattern density for 25-yard quail even with improved cylinder. Many light 20s, 16s and 12s have pretty open chokes. Point one of these at a tight covey of $5,000-bobwhites, and you're likely to fringe a bird you didn't intend to. That same plantation has an unspoken rule that anybody who shoots more than two birds in a covey, whether they intended to or not, will never be invited back. And it is enforced. In the Dakotas the pheasant may put the "bird" in bird hunting, and up in New England the ruffed grouse may be the king of gamebirds, but south of the Mason-Dixon Line the quail is Gentleman Bob, and you will hunt him like a gentleman or never darken their door again.

The classic bobwhite gun for such exclusive plantations is a double, preferably side-by-side. On the exclusive wild quail plantations this gun will be riding in a fancy leather scabbard on a smooth-gaited horse. But for plain old quail hunters, those who either walk miles for one or two wild coveys or pay a few bucks for

Brush bobwhites take off.

pen-raised birds, a light pump or autoloader is often the choice. I have shot bobwhite quail with everything from a 28-gauge over-under to a 12-gauge autoloader chambered for the 3½-inch shell, and they all work as long as you point them right. If you are walking a lot, instead of riding, a light gun is much more comfortable.

A light gun also works better on those frequent occasions when bobwhites head for the brush. I have chased them into brush and timber that, while not terrifying to the average Michigan grouse hunter, still allow a quail to escape without a shot fired if you are not very quick. In such cover any gun much over 6½ pounds simply points too slowly for most hunters.

But light guns can also be too quick. On one covey along the brushy edge of a hayfield, a friend moved up through the brush and flushed the birds, hoping they'd fly into the field. I was standing a little to the right, holding my short little AyA sidelock. Most of the birds, of course, refused to fly into the open, instead scattering to either side around my friend, then buzzing toward the brush, so they had to be shot quickly. I picked out a bird and shot instinctively, just raising the shotgun and pulling the trigger. Unfortunately, the quail was flying right at me, instead of away, and though the shot connected, the result was a pair of wings, helicoptering to the ground like dead leaves, about 8 feet from my feet. We looked, but never did find a trace of the body. Since then I have decided not to try to push quail into the open because they rarely fly that way anyway. I'll take my chances on getting a shot before they zip around a myrtle bush.

Most shots at Southern bobwhites come at slight angles, with a few dead straight-aways thrown in. But there can be true crossing shots, where very muzzle-light shotguns are at a disadvantage. And though most shots measure less than 25 yards, once in a while you'll get a chance at a bird, especially from a wild covey, at 30 or 35. All things considered, I'll take my 16-gauge Beretta side-by-side, shooting an ounce of #7½ shot out of its loose improved-cylinder and tight modified barrels. Some folks prefer 8's, but here I agree with old-

A bobwhite about to meet some #7½ shot at White Oak Plantation in Alabama.

Alabama dog handler Marion
Davies and friend, White
Oak Plantation.

Pointer retrieving an Alabama bobwhite.

A pretty point in bobwhite country.

West of bobwhite country you run into both scaled and
Gambel's quail in the grasslands and cactus of the Southwest.

time Idaho cowboy/hunter Elmer Keith, who wrote that he'd just as soon never fire anything smaller than 7½'s at any gamebird. While 8's will definitely kill bobwhite quail out to normal ranges of 25 yards, past that 7½'s penetrate much better. Southern dog trainer and guide Marion Davies, who has seen about as many quail killed in his 39 years as anybody, says in open country he likes a load of 6's in the tight barrel, for long shots (a choice echoed by Arizona quail guide Web Parton). But I suspect that's because many of the hunters Marion guides on Whiteout Oak Plantation use the standard cheap "dove and quail" loads, with relatively soft shot. Target loads or handloads with hard shot provide plenty of penetration with 7½'s, out to the limits of quail range. If all your shots come at under 25 yards, use whatever shot you want from #6 to #8, but past 25 I would suggest hard 7½'s, both for its better penetration and denser patterns.

An ounce of shot is usually plenty, especially in a double that's choked improved cylinder and modified. Let's apply our density formula again. An ounce of 7½'s contains 350 pellets, and from an improved-cylinder choke almost all of these will land in a 30-inch circle at 20 yards. Our 700-square-inch circle ends up with a #7½ pellet in about every other square inch. Bobwhites have a vital area of about 6 square inches, which means an average of three shot per bird at that range. Acceptable, if not overwhelming—but unlike pheasants, bobwhite quail are not particularly tough to kill. Modified choke puts about all its shot into a 30-inch circle at 30 yards, at least with hard shot, so it provides clean kills at that range. If the shot load drops to around ¾ ounce, as it does in the .410 and 28-gauge, you either need to shorten your maximum ranges to less than 25 yards, or use more choke. A full-choke 28 will cleanly kill bobwhites at 30 yards or a bit more.

Let's move west now. While the bobwhite hunting in the Brush Country of South Texas tends to limit shots to close ranges, farther north in the Panhandle, and out on the prairies of Oklahoma the shots will be longer, and often complicated by wind. Here it's often a good idea to leave the .410s and 28s at home. As we've seen, at least an ounce of shot and modified choke is necessary for consistent kills at 30 yards. Many of the prairie quail hunters I know prefer a little more shot, say 1⅛ ounces, at least for the second shot, which requires "magnum" loads even in the 2¾ 20-gauge shell. And quite a few prefer full choke in the second barrel of doubles, especially toward the end of the season.

On the western edge of prairie bobwhite country, you start running into scaled, or blue, quail. These de-

mand even more of the same sort of gun and load, since scaled quail are known as runners wherever they're hunted. Web Parton says that with a pair of really good dogs and some decent grass (hard to find in the overgrazed Southwest) scaled quail hold quite well. But no matter the quality of the dogs or cover, shots at scaled quail do tend to run longer than on the average bobwhite in Georgia. I have shot blue quail with 1¼-ounce loads in the improved-modified choke of my old 97 Winchester and never felt a twinge of guilt. I'd probably be hung anywhere in the old Confederacy for shooting bobwhites with the same gun.

Farther west is the desert quail country of New Mexico and Arizona. Here you'll still find scaled quail anywhere you still find patches of prairie, but you also find Gambel's and Mearns quail. Each of these presents its own specific problems. Gambel's live in the true Sonoran desert, where almost everything has thorns, sometimes even the grass. In good years, when the rains come at the right times, the birds can seemingly be everywhere, but in drier years you can follow a pointing dog for a long time through the ocotillo, cholla and palo verde.

Gambel's don't hold as well as southern bobwhites, and not nearly as well as the Mearns, which often would rather squat than fly. While Gambel's are almost always found around cover that's head-high or better, its also fairly open cover. So shots can come at any range from 10 yards to infinity, though most are under 30 yards, since the birds usually find a thorny something to dive over or around by that range. In sparse years, when you must make the most of any chance you get, I like a 20- or 16-gauge, loaded with at least an ounce of 7½'s, preferably a double-barrel choked improved-cylinder and modified. But a good repeater choked modified is not a bad choice. In one year of particularly hard walking, I really learned to appreciate the 5½ pounds of my dear departed Franchi 20-gauge autoloader. With the modified choke tube, it would take 15-yard birds if I pointed precisely, and still drop 35-yard Gambel's cleanly. Occasionally you'll have the opportunity for a third shot on Gambel's quail because, like prairie grouse, a straggler or two can flush after the main covey has flown and you've already blown both chances with your fancy side-by-side. But whatever gun you choose, use hard shot and plenty of it. Gambel's are pretty tough birds, and if they hit the ground alive, they can wiggle into a prickly pear or cholla patch and be gone forever.

Mearns are completely different. For one thing, despite being noticeably larger than Gambel's quail (which are about the size of a bobwhite) they have the reputation of being not near as tough. Or is this be-

cause they're big enough that the same pattern density tends to put another pellet or two in a Mearns? They hold very well—indeed they're almost impossible to find without a dog, since they rarely flush even if somebody walks within a few feet—and live in more benign surroundings than the Gambel's. The high oak-and-grass hills of southeastern Arizona's Mearns country are some of the prettiest upland bird habitat anywhere, looking more like the central valley foothills of California than the desert. So Mearns don't have much cactus to crawl under.

Whatever. It just doesn't take as much shot to kill a Mearns, but it does take a very quick shotgun. Last December Web Parton guided me and Eileen after these exotic quail down near Sonoita. We left Web's home in Oracle in the dark, driving toward Mexico. South of Tucson the sun rose and the country opened up into those beautiful rolling oak hills. Off in the distance the Sierrita Mountains rose toward a line of thunderheads, both blue mountains and gray clouds precisely visible even dozens of miles away. After trying a couple of Web's favorite canyons and finding either the grass eaten to the ground, or evidence of people who might not have legally entered the United States, we finally found the right spot late in the afternoon. We hiked a few miles across the grassy ridges and down into the more lush valleys, the dogs circling ahead along the edges of the blue oaks that shaded the slopes.

After a couple hours of this, Eileen's asthma had just about had it, so she kept to one of the little valleys while Web and I circled the ridges above. And that was where the dogs went on point, on the edge of a side-draw just where the hill curved down, a few feet from a lone pinyon pine. The dogs stood like two white compasses converging toward magnetic north, which seemed to be located in a little patch of grass about 5 feet in front of their noses.

"Move in slowly," Web said. "Right at that grass."

So I did, holding the 16 lightly. Nothing happened. Web clucked at the lead dog and it moved up, pointing again closer to the tree. Web whispered, "I'll move in."

"Okay," I said, "let me get up the hill, in case they fly that way."

Gambel's quail live in mixed brush and grassland. These two were taken with a light Beretta 20-gauge over-under, choked cylinder and modified, a perfect choice for varied quail shooting.

Gambel's quail north of Tucson.

He nodded, then eased forward, whispering to the dog. They shuffled that way for a minute or more, a few inches at a time, until Web leaned far forward and looked directly down at the ground in front of him, near the lower branches of the tree. "They're right underneath me. Ready?"

I nodded, and when Web scuffled one small step forward, birds sprayed into the air like feathered drops from a fountain. I picked out one dark bird in the main covey as they tried to fly around the tree, and shot with the open barrel. It seemed to lurch, but in any case most of the covey was already around the tree, so I swung to the left and shot at a lone bird that had flown that way, and it fell. "I think I got two," I said, not sure about the first one, since everything had taken so long and yet happened so fast.

Web was already picking up the birds, two males. Both fell no more than 15 yards from my feet. "Aren't they incredible?" he said, holding the black-and white birds high. They looked like a pair of miniature guinea fowl. I nodded, out of words, and then we followed the singles down through the trees, shooting at them like little ruffed grouse as they twisted through the oaks.

So from my limited experience with Mearns, and Web's long experience with them, I would say an open choke is a good idea. They hold well.

North and west of Arizona are found the California valley quail and the larger mountain quail. Their habitat stretches all the way up to southern British Columbia. Closely resembling Gambel's, the valley quail presents the same problems. But instead of living in cactus they prefer sagebrush, or the low brush along stream courses, or in southern California, rolling oak hills much like the Mearns country. But the shots seem exactly the same as those at Gambel's, varying from very close to as far as you can shoot. Shoot quickly when they get up around brush because they'll dive right back in a few yards later.

Mountain quail live in, well, mountains, or at least on the edges of them. They've grown more scarce over their entire range in the past couple of decades, and indeed there's no longer a season in some areas. Where you can still hunt mountain quail, the shooting tends to be closer and quicker than for either Gambel's or valley quail, simply because mountain quail live in thicker cover. They're a bigger bird too, if not any

Doves flying against the afternoon sky.

Watering a desert quail dog.

tougher than the smaller birds. Use the same gun you would on Mearns, with more open chokes than you'd choose for the open-country quail.

The quail-gun picture gets clouded by other game-birds, though, the farther north you travel in the Midwest and West. In Arizona or southern California, the only other bird you might encounter at the same time would be doves, but farther north and east on the plains you might run into prairie chickens and sharp-tailed grouse. In the high West you'll also find Hungarian and chukar partridge, band-tailed pigeons, and even ruffed and blue grouse. And anywhere north of Oklahoma, Arizona or California you might run into a rooster pheasant. The safe thing to do, of course, is carry a gun and load adequate for the biggest bird you might encounter, while trying to provide for enough pattern density for quail. I tend to carry at least a 20 or 16, with some shells loaded with 6's and others with 7½'s, switching loads if possible. But the 6's ride in the gun most of the time, and at least 1⅛ ounces of them.

The other frequently hunted small upland bird over most of North America is the mourning dove, with the similar whitewing also popular in the Southwest. Doves are even smaller than quail, and the shots are frequently longer. They're also harder to hit, on average, especially when flying high heading back to their roost, or shifting in the air around farm fields. Combine the difficulty of the shooting with the normally high daily limit—often 15 birds—and a lot of banging sometimes takes place.

The ideal dove gun is many contradictory things. Bob Brister once said as we sat around a dove field: "It's got to be light and responsive, to catch up to the little bastards. But it's also got to swing well and kick lightly. Hitting 'em's easier with an open choke, but you kill more cleanly with a tight choke, especially when they're flying high." Which means a light, long, soft-kicking shotgun with a wide, high-density pattern. Got that?

Actually, there are at least three common methods

138

of dove shooting, which mean differences in dove guns. They're most commonly shot when flying in and around farm fields. Here the shots can come in any variety from low and slow to high and fast. This implies some versatility, either a double, choked improved cylinder and whatever tighter choke you like, or a repeater choked modified. Some double shooters prefer #8 shot in the loose barrel and #7½ in the tight choke, on the theory that high birds require more pellet energy and penetration. Sometimes this even works. But even on doves I like #7½'s, just because they penetrate better at long range. A dove isn't that much smaller than a quail, and while they can be pretty tough to bring down, one #7½ in the right place will do the job; with 350 shot in an ounce of #7½'s versus around 410 in an ounce of 8's, there isn't all that much difference in pattern density. (Some dove hunters even choose #9 shot, because there are close to 600 in an ounce. But they simply don't penetrate consistently past 20 yards. Unless all your shots come at very close range—where even 6's would provide enough pattern density—forget about "dust" shot.)

Whatever shot size, target loads with hard shot definitely work better on doves than the so-called "dove and quail" loads. You want all the pattern density you can get. And if you buy by the case, sharing with a buddy or two, the cost per box isn't that much more than the cheap stuff. The ammunition companies make lots of target ammo every year, so 20- and 12-gauge loads are pretty cheap. The problem gauges are 28 and 16. Not nearly as many 28s are sold every year as 20s, so 28s cost a little more, even though they're smaller. And there simply isn't a commercial 16-gauge target load made, since nobody shoots them in registered target games. But if you love the 16 you probably handload anyway. Just buy hard shot, and stuff at least an ounce of it in each shell.

For field shooting a medium-gauge double might be best. The 28 is astonishing on doves, killing almost as far as a 20, and kicks noticeably less. In a 16 or 12, a

Reporting the hunt in southern Arizona.

repeater works just about as well, but with the smaller gauges I'd stick with a double for the choice in chokes. You really need a tight modified or even full choke to kill the higher doves with a 28 or even a standard 20.

A similar dove-hunting technique involves shooting over waterholes as the birds come in to drink. This is typically done in the dry West, and usually a close-range affair, which implies a lighter, open-choked more responsive gun. The typical quail gun is just about perfect. I like a little more pattern density than a .410 can provide, but an awful lot of waterhole doves are killed with .410s every year. The 28 seems to be a much better choice, however, and a 20 is really all you need.

Probably the second most common method of dove shooting is while they're flying back to roost in the evening. Here almost all the shots are long, so the birds are not nearly so evasive. So a bigger, tight-choked, smoother-swing gun works better. I will take at least a 20-gauge for high-flying roosting birds, however, and am not at all ashamed to shoot a 12, and preferably an autoloader. A couple of years ago in Argentina several of us shot the first evening at a roosting flight near the Parana River. A good wind was blowing behind them that evening and the birds flew high and very fast. I chose some $1\frac{1}{8}$-ounce high-velocity trap loads and my old Remington 870 with modified choke, and was not even close to being over-gunned. The birds flew so fast that it took about a dozen shots just to find the lead, which looked to be at least 15 feet. Sometimes birds would whoosh by and I'd never catch up to them, just swing the muzzle and forget about it. And very often I'd swing at the front bird in a flock and kill two or three birds a few feet behind the leader. Full choke would not have been out of line, and by sunset I was wishing for an autoloader's softer kick. According to my guide, sitting behind me and counting, I killed 62 birds that evening, which is actually nothing down there, where doves are considered agricultural predators in many areas and there are no limits. But my bird-per-shell average was not high, even with a few multiple-bird shots, since six boxes of empty shells lay on the ground. Shooting 150 high-velocity loads in less than an hour can take it right out of your shoulder.

Most American dove hunting doesn't require that

Mearns quail tend to hold very tightly, so your gun has to be quick. These were taken with a light 16-gauge Beretta side-by-side, using an ounce of #7$\frac{1}{2}$ shot.

This is typical valley quail country in southwestern Idaho. The classic quail gun will work fine here, but you may also flush a chukar partridge or rooster pheasant from the same draw, so your shells should be loaded with #6 shot.

much shooting, thank goodness. But I've seen shooters use three or four boxes to take a 15-bird limit. An autoloader is definitely more comfortable for that much shooting of a 12-gauge load, or even lighter loads for some recoil-sensitive shooters.

Some hunters ask why I shoot such small birds as doves and quail when there's hardly any meat on them. My answer is that what meat there is tastes as fine as any wild or tame flesh on earth. They're easy to pluck, and in many years the fertile and abundant little birds reproduce so much that they seem to cover the countryside. In those autumns, taking some for the table is not just a pleasure but a celebration of the circle of life.

The dove gun must be many contradictory things: light and responsive, yet hard-hitting and smooth-swinging. These shooters chose an autoloader and over-under.

CHAPTER EIGHT

FOREST BIRDS

To many eastern wingshooters the ruffed grouse and woodcock are the only forest gamebirds, but others do live in North America. Though some hunters would dispute the "gamebird" moniker being attached to the spruce grouse, the "fool hen" of the north. Still, places exist where spruce grouse are not only avidly hunted, but pursued with pointing dogs and side-by-side shotguns. In the Rocky Mountains, from northern New Mexico and Arizona up into the Yukon, lives the blue grouse, which some would claim is the king of forest gamebirds, since it grows to twice the size of the ruffed grouse, with the same delicate white flesh. And the ruffed grouse itself is not just a bird of Vermont briar thickets, but lives in quaking aspen stands in Utah and shares willow patches with ptarmigan in Alaska.

While an eastern chauvinist might admit that some sort of bird resembling the ruffed grouse lives in the West, they're not really the ultra-wary birds hunted in Pennsylvania or Michigan. Eastern grouse hunters often speak of having "moved" a certain number of birds in a day's hunt; grouse that whirred off heard but unseen. While it's true the other forest grouse often stand around like feathered diplomats when chanced upon by hikers or big game hunters—the source of their fool hen reputation, which often follows not only the spruce grouse but also the blue grouse and even western ruffs. But put a dog on the ground and all three birds change.

Even the most innocent British Columbia spruce grouse recognizes the general form of coyote, and none of our hunting dogs have evolved far enough from their wolf-dog ancestors to fool even a fool hen. The sudden, aggressive appearance of a four-footed, flop-eared, panting predator says "fly away, now" even to birds that have never seen a human before. And when they fly we can shoot them with shotguns.

Before we get into the right and proper sort of shotgun for forest grouse, I must make a confession. It is a long-standing Western tradition to shoot forest grouse with whatever hunting arm you have at hand, and that includes rifles and handguns. I gather this is even traditional in such eastern semi-wilderness as Maine. Indeed my friend Sherby Morris, who lives in Fort Kent at the very uppermost tip of that state, says flatly that it is not possible to kill Maine grouse with a shotgun, because the trees are too gosh-darn thick. (Sherby actually says things like gosh-

A shotgun for forest birds must be quick, light and open choked.

To many hunters, ruffed grouse are the only forest bird, and the king of all upland birds

146

darn, by the way.) So the primary grouse gun up there and out here is often a .22 rifle or handgun. In Montana a young hunter's first legal game is often a ruffed grouse shot off the edge of a logging track with dad's old rimfire. Over a period of 30-odd years I have not only killed mountain grouse with .22 rifles and revolvers, but various .270s and .30-06s and even arrows. All of this is perfectly legal; our hunting regulations specifically state that while only shotguns and archery tackle are legal for taking prairie birds, rifles and handguns are legal on mountain grouse. It is a real hunting tradition, not just rednecks whacking meat from their pickup window.

I must also emphasize that shooting a ruffed grouse out of a tree with a Colt revolver, or taking a blue's head off with a 180-grain elk bullet is not nearly as easy as it sounds, and in some ways is just as "sporting" (however that word is defined) as shooting them on the wing with a scatter-gun that spreads its shot over a three-foot circle.

More than a decade ago, I once mentioned this very thing in a magazine article, saying that I fully expected some snobs to call me names for shooting the King of Gamebirds while it sat in a tree. Well, I have done it and will do it again and have probably killed nearly as many mountain grouse with bullets as dog and shotgun. If you object, let's meet up at Cabin Gulch in the Elkhorn Mountains next October 1st,

and duel it out. You get to use your Parker or L.C. Smith or whatever New England grouse gun you choose, while I aim my custom .270.

Enough of that. While I welcome a mountain grouse meal, no matter what kind of hole there is through the bird, dog-and-shotgun remains the most pleasurable way to catch them. The classic New England ruffed grouse gun is, of course, a side-by-side. A very few choose a .410, a few more a 28-gauge, but the vast majority of eastern ruffed grouse hunters prefer something from 20- to 12-gauge. It just has to be open-choked, because the typical shot is at grouse fleetingly seen through the trees.

I will agree that a double-gun is perhaps the best all-around forest shotgun but not that it needs to be totally open-choked. Yes, one barrel should be open, preferably straight cylinder. But the second barrel should be fairly tight. Aside from aesthetics, the only real reason to carry a double is for a choice of chokes. You can get the same sort of light weight and smooth balance in a repeater, if you just know where to look. So why handicap yourself with a double that has both barrels bored wide-open?

But why, you counter, would any hunter need a tight choke in thick woods? The longest shot might be 30 yards, and is usually much less, especially before the leaves fall from the trees. Well, because you're often shooting not just between but *through* those

Cooling off the Labrador on a mountain grouse hunt.

A ruffed grouse that flew into the open.

trees, and especially leaves. While often an opening can be picked, the only consistent way to hit forest grouse is to mount and swing and pull the trigger, whether the bird is flying between or behind the trees. If you attempt to pick and choose the moment, your swing will stall out and you'll miss. Believe me, I know.

The best choke for shooting through twigs and leaves is something much tighter than cylinder or even improved cylinder. An open choke's pattern is sparse enough without half the shot being stopped by vegetation. Once you send the shot from a tight modified or full pattern through an aspen or conifer branch, its pattern ends up about as sparse as the spread from a more open choke.

Some hunters try to combat this by using finer shot, but even a ruffed grouse is pretty hefty, most mature birds weighing $1\frac{1}{2}$ pounds or so. That's much bigger than any quail, so #7$\frac{1}{2}$ shot doesn't quite have enough penetration, every time. Sure, ranges are short, but with the quick shooting through all the obstacles, birds are often hit with only one or two pellets. Number six shot hits a lot harder than #7$\frac{1}{2}$'s, and since the ranges are normally short, pattern density is quite adequate. At 20 yards even a true cylinder pattern usually falls entirely within a 30-inch circle. With an ounce of #6's, that means at least three pellets in the 10-square-inch vital area of a ruffed grouse.

And with the tighter barrel, pattern density is tremendous. My recent grouse doubles all have a tighter barrel choked at least 15 points, which with good hard shot usually puts the shot into 24 inches at 25 yards. The area of a 24-inch circle is about 450 square inches, meaning an ounce of #6's (225 shot) will put five pellets into a ruffed grouse at that range. Even if you lose 40 percent of the pattern to an aspen

Open chokes work for very close shots, but tighter chokes do better when shooting through brush. This grouse hunter used a modified choke in his pumpgun.

branch, that's three pellets in the bird.

It's amazing what can be done with a tight barrel in thick cover. Last fall I was hunting an east-facing mountainside covered by mixed conifers and occasional aspen thickets, the chocolate Lab working ahead of me between a big aspen patch and a line of pines. After a few minutes he started snuffling back toward me, and a gray ruffed grouse flushed almost exactly between us, headed for the pines. I threw up the 16-gauge Beretta and pulled the left trigger as the bird disappeared behind a big branch, and saw the branch shudder as the shot tore through. *So much for that bird*, I thought, since hardly any light could be seen between the needles. But about 15 seconds later the old dog appeared with a totally defunct grouse in its mouth. When I plucked the bird a few days later there were four #6 shot in its body.

Spruce grouse are slightly smaller than ruffs, though not enough to matter. But blues are something else, the biggest birds are slightly larger than a rooster pheasant, if not nearly as tough. This can actually be felt when eating one. The skin simply isn't as tough as a pheasant's, and even old males chew only half as hard as a ringneck. So the shot doesn't have as much resistance, and the ranges tend to be closer. Since the target is bigger than a ruffed grouse, more shot is likely to hit the bird. I've found the same ounce of #6 shot

A Boykin spaniel, side-by-side 20-gauge and a ruffed grouse.

to be totally adequate for blues, but if you want to be really sure add another $\frac{1}{8}$ ounce.

A double gun seems truly the right gun to have in hand, even when after spruce grouse and blues. This is at least partly because this is one form of wingshooting where good gun fit not only helps, but is absolutely essential. Even if you've never been trained in instinctive shooting, that's what shooting grouse through trees amounts to. When a forest grouse flushes you might have two or three seconds to mount the gun and shoot, so there's no time for looking finely down the rib and making minute adjustments. If the gun isn't lined up the moment it hits your shoulder it never will be. Light doubles tend to come up this way more frequently than the average repeater. Add the choice of chokes, and the double seems the only real choice.

But this doesn't mean there isn't a place in the forest for repeaters. Many seasons open pretty early in the fall, when the birds are often still in family coveys—our Montana season, for instance, starts September 1st. When flushed, the main bunch may thunder off, scattering across a hillside, often a bird or two waits to see what happens. Maybe it had its head down, pecking at a grasshopper, when everybody else left, and is now trying to locate the rest of the flock. I have emptied a double without result at departing September ruffs or blues several times, then had one or two more birds whir away.

So early in the season the gun of choice is often a repeater. The Franchi 20-gauge autoloader is perfect for this, despite the somewhat tighter choke tubes typical in European guns. As noted above, sometimes a tighter pattern helps, especially on second shots as the birds twist through the trees. For forest grouse I often load one spreader load in the chamber, either a cheap factory load or an actual spreader, then harder shot in the shells behind. My Franchi's "improved cylinder" choke tube actually measured .009 inches of constriction, which verges on modified in the 20-gauge, and worked very well with the combination of shells described above. Since selling the Franchi I've started using my 6¼-pound Winchester Model 12 16-gauge for the same job. This old pumpgun has a 26-inch barrel marked modified, but the actual choke is .010 inches of constriction, and patterns about the same as the Franchi did, though with a little more punch.

The classic ruffed grouse shotgun is a side-by-side, which is exactly what the author chose many years ago to take this gray-phase bird in western Montana.

These are tighter chokes than usually advised for ruffed grouse, but I like their versatility, both for the occasional longer shot and shooting through trees. My first really dedicated grouse gun was a Savage 20-gauge pumpgun that I bought in a hardware store in Wolf Point, Montana, back in the mid-70s. It had a 28-inch full-choked barrel, the typical cowboy-country shotgun for laying across the gun rack in the

pickup window. I shot a few pheasants with it and wasn't entirely impressed.

A few months later I happened to read Frank Woolner's excellent book, *Grouse and Grouse Hunting*. Though written totally about eastern ruffed grouse, it held some excellent information about grouse guns, especially Woolner's own modifications of several, and he wasn't bound by the eastern double-gun tradition. One of his favorite grouse guns was a Winchester Win-Lite Model 59 autoloader. This gun was well ahead of its time, gas-operated with a barrel consisting of a thin steel liner wound inside fiberglass strands. It was very light, and Woolner made it lighter, both by slimming the forend and cutting the barrel to 23 inches, leaving it without any choke at all. It weighed six pounds and handled, Woolner claimed, just right in the grouse woods. (This gun was also the first on the market with screw-in chokes. Woolner kept a second barrel so equipped for other hunting, but like the fiberglass barrel, the chokes were too far ahead of their time. I suspect Frank would grin now if he could see the standardization of screw-in choke tubes.)

After reading Woolner, I grew unsatisfied with my cowboy pumpgun, and hacksawed the barrel of the Savage to 23 inches and refitted the front sight. Thus lobotomized, it weighed just about six pounds, so I took it not only ruffed grouse hunting but after early-season sharp-tails and Huns as well. It was incredibly easy to hit with, except for two things. It now shot very high, the bottom of the pattern barely overlapping the barrel when I cheeked the gun, and the wide-open spread was a little dicey on ruffed grouse at 30 yards. As my evolution as a forest grouse hunter progressed, I came to reserve cylinder "choke" for the right barrel of side-by-sides, so there would be a choice if needed. And I began to have my doubts about the standard advice for a high-shooting upland gun.

Of course, the Savage shot too damned high. The traditional forest grouse gun is also supposed to shoot just a little high, maybe 6 inches at 25 yards, since the birds should be rising at the shot. But an awful lot of ruffed and blue grouse hunting takes place in steep country. Blues in particular like to fly straight downhill, and I've seen ruffs sail downslope frequently, or at least along the side of a hill down around a ridge. A high-shooting gun will cause misses at falling birds.

There is a theory that a side-by-side works better in the dim woods than any single-plane gun. The light is relatively poor, so the broad muzzles of a side-by-side show up better. I guess so, and it's probably truer the older we get. But the real reason behind this theory probably involves deep-seated New England prejudices against the upstart over-under, or those damn rackety repeaters. I tend to pick a side-by-side because of the twin triggers and instant choice of chokes. If over-unders had two triggers I'd just as soon carry one.

The ruffed grouse gun works for woodcock—or so I have been told. These are the one gamebird in this book I've never laid eyes on, though I have frequently gunned their marsh cousin, the snipe. In the interests of journalistic balance and objectivity I tried all last fall to shoot a woodcock. Initially I imposed myself on my friend Tony Dolle, weaseling an invitation on the early October trip he and several friends make each year to Michigan's Upper Peninsula. The main object of this expedition is ruffed grouse, but the timing hopes to coincide with the woodcock migration. But then I got invited on an all-expenses-paid elk hunt in New Mexico, and foolishly accepted. I never saw an elk, but Tony was kind enough to schedule another woodcock trip for mid-November, when the 'cocks would theoretically be in an area of southern Missouri Tony knows well. We would hunt with the state woodcock biologist, and it sounded great.

Except for one thing. Deer season, it turned out, opened the same weekend, and the three of us agreed that we'd just as soon not be following dogs through thick cover while thousands of rifle-shooters hit the woods. But that was okay, since I was planning a duck hunt in Mississippi in the second week of January, and my host down there said the woodcock would be in then, and he knew where to find them. But during the first week of January, the biggest blizzard to hit the Midwest in years blew through. It didn't snow in Mississippi, but the woodcock swamps froze, and they left.

So, I never did find a damned woodcock. According to some of my friends this is just as well, but here I must rely on the expertise of Tony Dolle. He says woodcock hunting involves crashing through really thick brush like a Sherman tank, then every once in a while vaguely sighting something that flies like a big butterfly with a bunch of feathers stuck up its butt. At that point the Sherman tank must try to untangle its cannon from the trees and shoot. This doesn't work very often, so when on the rare occasions that one of the butterflies rises in a small opening, the tank misses completely. Tony says since woodcock are pretty small—not much bigger than a dove—that some people choose #9 shot for their cannons, but at the very close ranges of typical woodcock hunting #7$\frac{1}{2}$ works just as well, and does much better than the 9's on the ruffed grouse that show up between butterflies.

But whatever forest shotgun you choose, whether for ruffed grouse in New England, spruce grouse on the Alaska Peninsula, blues in Wyoming, or woodcock wherever the things exist (and they must live somewhere; I've seen photos) it must be light. This helps you shoot quickly and walk farther, especially through the typical knee-grabbing cover of ruffed grouse, or along the 9,000-foot ponderosa ridges that blue grouse often inhabit.

Abject poverty has forced me to lug a few shotguns that weighed more than 7 pounds after forest grouse, but in these days of mere semi-poverty I much prefer something less than 6$\frac{3}{4}$ pounds, and even lighter does not hurt my feelings. When hunting forest birds its not just the walking that wears you out, but the constant handling of the gun. It often must be carried in one hand while you push aside brush, and must always be in at least two hands, across your chest and ready to shoot. Unlike open-country upland hunting, where the gun can be carried across a shoulder or sometimes even slung, the shots come too quickly for anything but port-arms. As mentioned earlier, studies have shown that weights carried by our extremities—the shotguns in our hands or boots on our feet—tend to tire us more than the same weight slung over our shoulders or tied around our waists. So make that grouse gun light, and preferably not too muzzle-heavy. Along about mid-afternoon you will grow extremely tired of carrying a muzzle-heavy gun in one hand, even if it only weighs 6 pounds.

Ruffed grouse cover in western Montana.

A covey of Hungarian partridge flushing from the wheat stubble.

Up close, they appear as delicate brick-and-slate paintings that rest beautifully in the hand. Plus, like the legendary trombone-action shotgun, I have never heard any hunter say "gray partridge" unless forced to by outside influences.

Huns are much like a twice-as-big prairie version of the bobwhite quail. They live in coveys that generally number 10 or a dozen birds early in fall, and at that time of year hold pretty well for a pointing dog. They really love wheat and other small-grain fields, so much that despite their range overlapping that of many other prairie birds, you can often hunt Huns almost exclusively by sticking to the stubble, ignoring all that trashy pheasant cover around the edges. A great many Hun enthusiasts do this, partly because they prefer a covey rising in front of a pointing dog, and partly because they prefer to carry light little shotguns.

For a pure early-season Hun gun, the 28-gauge works perfectly and indeed may be the one real use for the little gauge on the northern prairies. (Forget the .410. It simply patterns too raggedly for open country. Most people who try it stretch their shooting ranges—after all, you can still see the birds flying away—and wound more than a few.) But as the season progresses and the birds get bigger, tougher and wilder I have found the 28 to be less than ideal. Most September birds are probably shot at 30 yards or less, while shots of more than 30 yards are common later on. Past the middle of October a Hun becomes a pretty tough bird. I have seen them take a 12-gauge load of #7½ shot and fly 100 yards before falling. Number 6 shot tends to work better later on, with tighter chokes. Use plenty of shot; a Hun only has a vital area of about 8 square inches. Plus, unless you're a real wheatfield purist, you're likely to flush bigger birds like chukars, sharp-tails or even pheasants and sage grouse while out on a Hun walk.

Whether you carry a double or repeater is up to

159

you, but I often choose a pumpgun, especially early, when a straggler can come up after the main covey. I'll also carry a pumpgun really late, when the birds get up farther out and one tight choke beats two loose-and-tight chokes. Of course, if your double is equipped with choke tubes you can screw in two fulls. It is possible, if not easy, to triple on a covey of Huns with a pump or autoloader, but this becomes more likely if you don't shoot like a double-gunner. Shooters who habitually carry two-barreled guns normally take the easiest bird (i.e.—closest bird) first with their open barrel, then swing on the rapidly disappearing covey and give the next-easiest bird a try with their tighter barrel. Supposedly this is one of the reasons for a double: an open choke for the first shot, a tight choke for the second, farther shot.

Try this with a pump or autoloader and the third bird will be too far away, unless they got up awfully close or you're awfully quick. Plus, you should be using a tighter choke, at least modified, and it's the only one you've got. So pick out a bird at the front of the covey and shoot him first. This actually makes hitting easier, since the pattern has a chance to spread a bit more. When that bird falls, it will (of course) try for another leading bird. Only on the third shot should you try for a trailing bird.

I really like a light repeater on that other imported partridge, the chukar. These don't hold nearly as well as Huns, even early in the season, and often run and scatter across those damned rocky Idaho ridges. By the time you chase them around for an hour or so trying to get one to flush, you're likely to whack away at any bird that gets up within even long range. As soon as you shoot twice with your double gun (the second shot was useless—you knew that—but it felt good to blast something, even if it was just sky) another bird will flush a mere 15 yards from your aching feet and slide down the mountain within easy range while you stand there with an empty gun.

Chukar are enough bigger than Huns to definitely need #6 shot. I like at least modified choke, and while a Hun gun is more fun to carry and shoot when it's light, a 7-pounder isn't unreasonable. Unless you're built like Hulk Hogan, you will not like carrying a shotgun that heavy up a chukar ridge, no matter how pretty and well-balanced the gun may be. Though I have killed chukars with guns as varied as a 6-pound 28-gauge Browning Citori over-under and my old Remington 870 with the modified barrel, my favorite chukar gun these days is the 6$\frac{1}{4}$-pound 16-gauge Model 12 Winchester pump I bought from Steve Bodio a few seasons back. It seems to be exactly the right combination of weight and firepower. And it hits

The author's favorite chukar gun is a 6¹/₄-pound Winchester Model 12 in 16-gauge. Late-season birds can take a lot of shot, provided by Federal's Premium 1¹/₄ ounce magnum load.

plenty hard. You do want to hit chukars hard. The shots can be tough, at any angle and range, and if a lightly hit bird sails on set wings down one of those canyons, you will be extremely sorry. I prefer to stop my chukars where they're hit. Since the shots can be long, I like more than an ounce of shot, so late in the season I am not shy about using $1\frac{1}{4}$ ounces of good hard 6's.

This little 16 is also my favorite early-season sharp-tail and prairie chicken gun. From September up until about mid-October both these birds hold pretty well, but flush raggedly, where the extra shots come in handy. At least they hold well if you wait until a civilized hour to go chasing them. When I was "cowboying" on an eastern Montana ranch just out of high school, the traditional way to hunt sharp-tails was to rise early in the morning and drive out to a newly-harvested wheatfield at dawn, spilling coffee in your lap the whole way, then form a skirmish line of hunters and dogs and advance on the birds feeding in the field. But even September sharp-tails don't like to see six hunters and three dogs walking their way across the shorn stubble, so 99 percent took off at long range.

A chukar gun must be light, since the country is so steep. This hunter carries a light 12-gauge into the chukar hills along the Oregon-Idaho border.

162

When they left the fields they flew into the brushy draws dropping off into the draws along the edges of the fields. These areas were usually full of chokecherry, buffalo-berry and wild roses. By the time we got done driving all the birds off the stubble, the sun would be well up and the day warming. The combination of cover and heat would hold the birds in the draws, where the dogs would push them up 10 or 20 yards in front of our guns. This always seemed to be more sensible to me, even at 17, so when I got old enough to have the inner strength to resist tradition, I started sleeping in until sunrise, getting up and eating a leisurely breakfast, and going out and flushing my sharptails out of the brush at close range, rather than at .270 range across the wheat stubble.

For this sort of work a light repeater works just fine. The shooting isn't difficult, so even a 28 will work if you have the discipline to keep shots close. Many of the shots will be close, especially the singles.

But I prefer a 20- or 16-gauge, simply because it takes less dog work to round up dead birds instead of cripples, and the heat of September tires dogs quickly. The gun should also shoot about where you

A North Dakota sharp-tail draw in early October.

A typical sharp-tail draw on the high plains, which may also hold pheasants.

Many hunters prefer a repeater for sharp-tailed grouse and it shouldn't shoot too high, since many will be taken when flying below the hunter.

look, not slightly high in the classic upland manner, because a lot of shots will be below you as you walk the high sides of draws and shoot at birds coming out of the brush in the bottom. When you're used to these shots they're not too tough, but shooters accustomed to birds flushing at their level can have a hard time.

The first time I ever shot sporting clays was down in Mississippi back in the late 1980s, during the launch of the bird-hunting magazine *Shooting Sportsman*. The founder and owner was a corporate attorney from Oxford, Mississippi. (Yes, the Oxford of William Faulkner. The lawyer's house had once been owned by Faulkner's doctor, and one of the rooms downstairs overlooked the swimming pool. It was where Faulkner stayed when he was drying out from drinking binges. As the lawyer said, "And this is where William Faulkner passed out.")

This lawyer grew tired of being a rich lawyer and decided to buy a quail plantation and start a bird-hunting magazine. Soon he was broke. But before that happened some hunting writers were invited down for a big hoopla, part of which was shooting the clays layout on the plantation. Because it was May shooting real quail was not possible. In general I shot well for my first time out, but did spectacularly on the "Flushing Sharptail" station, where the shooter stood on the edge of a little draw and the targets flew from a trap in the bottom, angling up the draw. Wham, wham! I

Prairie grouse like to hang out around any sort of cover, even shelterbelts.

166

Sharp-tailed grouse roosting in a December ponderosa pine.

Two male sage grouse, about 12 pounds in your bird vest.

dropped every pair that flew, while my much more practiced shooting partners missed a few. They were amazed, but they were all quail and pheasant hunters, not used to shooting birds well below them.

I suspect their double guns also shot a bit high, which didn't help. A classic high-shooting gun tends to shoot even higher at birds well below the shooter, because no matter how well you cheek the gun, your head tends to remain more upright than when shooting at birds at the same level or above you. This raises your eye, making the gun shoot higher. I was shooting my old 870 pumpgun, which shot right where I looked, and just raised the gun until the barrel passed the clay bird and pulled the trigger. It was exactly like shooting a real sharp-tail.

Prairie chickens don't like heavy brush nearly as well as do sharp-tails. Instead, they stick to high grass or lower, thinner brush like the knee-high "buck-brush" that covers many shallow draws on the high prairies. But other than that, the shooting is very similar. I like #6 shot for any of the mid-size prairie grouse. Many native hunters like #4's, but many native hunters also like full choke. Well, maybe not "like," but they and their fathers and grandfather's have always purchased full choke pumps and autoloaders, so that's what they shoot. A full choke patterns #4's tightly enough for most prairie grouse shooting, though it's too much for close range. Modified choke and #6 shot work better on early birds. You'll hit more close birds, and not tear up their delicious breast meat.

Later on, when the birds gather up and grow spookier, use all the choke you can get. I still prefer #6's, though premium loads with hard shot really make a difference past 35 yards. And I still prefer a repeater. In November both sharp-tails and prairie chickens leave the lower cover, whether brushy draws or tall-

Early in the season sage grouse can be found around water, and aren't too tough to kill, even the big roosters weighing six pounds or more.

grass swales, and live more on top of the ridges. If you can get close to them at all (they'll sometimes flush at half a mile, particularly when there's snow on the ground) the typical situation is to walk over a ridge-knob and see a few grouse standing in the short grass 40 or more yards away. A lot of the time these birds will flush, and if you whang away with your double gun, 20 more will flush closer, from the ground just behind the ridge-curve that you can't see. Once again your empty double gun will be useless and since the big late-season coveys may include all the sharp-tails or chickens for several miles, you'd better shoot one or two of these birds, or go home with none. When a big covey takes off they often fly until they disappear against the gray November sky.

I've only had limited experience with ptarmigan, usually as a sideline on various big game hunts in the North, but have talked a lot to my friends in Alaska. The same shotguns and loads you'd carry for prairie grouse seem ideal. Ptarmigan also hold better early in the season, before their feathers turn white, and if there's any cover like willows or dwarf birch, they hide in there. Early-season birds also tend to flush raggedly, just like prairie grouse. Later on, when the birds have become almost as absent of color as the snow that covers the tundra, they group together and flush at greater distances. A light repeater in 20- or 16-gauge for early birds, probably choked modified, and a full-choked 12 for late-season shooting should work perfectly.

Of course, there's no real reason you can't use a double on any of these birds, and I have many times. In good years any of the prairie or tundra birds can seem as numerous as pen-raised quail. In the heat of September they sometimes seem almost as predictable and tight-holding. A light double in any gauge from 28 up will do the job quite nicely, and there's always another covey a half-mile further on. I would have a 28 choked modified and full, unless using Winchester's one-ounce loads (and maybe even then), but the others could be improved cylinder and modified,

October sage grouse flush.

Mile eight of a sage grouse walk.

though I'd like at least $1^1/8$ ounces of shot, even in the 20-gauge. Later on a 16 or 12 provides a real edge over a 20, even the 3-inch magnum. The chokes could still be improved cylinder and modified, but really good ammunition would become an absolute necessity in order to tighten the chokes to a functional modified and full.

None of this applies to the last and greatest of the open-country upland birds, the sage grouse. Not too many folks make time to hunt these giant grouse, especially natives of the West. Residents of the region normally complain about their bitter, sagey taste. But I have noticed that the folks who won't eat sage hens usually toss their birds (whether sage grouse, Huns, prairie chickens or pheasants) into the bed of the pickup ungutted to roll around back there with the Mountain Dew cans, irrigating shovel and spare tire, until they get home late that evening, after stopping at the local bar for beer and microwaved pizza. I have also noticed that such folks tend to cook their birds by frying them until they're nice and leathery.

While it's true that a big cock sage grouse tends to taste like sagebrush, if you gut him within 30 minutes of shooting, and rinse out the body cavity with cool water, the sage will be only a seasoning, and it won't be bitter. Age him in the bottom of the refrigerator for a week, then slice off the breasts and cook them fairly gently any way you like. After marinating in teriyaki sauce, a hot barbecue works great. But the legs of an old bird simply cannot be chewed unless they're boiled until the meat falls off, at which point they make great enchiladas. The younger birds taste great any way you cook them, if you like dark meat. Just don't overcook them. Young birds should also be cleaned quickly.

The other reason to hunt sage grouse involves space. There is no place more wild and free and just plain empty of people as the vast sage grouse plains. To some people the miles and miles of olive knee-brush can even be intimidating, but to me this land is as beautiful as any mountain valley, especially when

Partners contemplating the beginning of a long walk across the sagebrush.

Moon over a sage grouse.

Early-season sharp-tail retrieve.

off in the distance you can often see blue mountains dancing lightly, as if seen through a very slight sheen of moving water. Since a great deal of the sagebrush plains are owned by you and me, the American public, you can walk almost anywhere you damn please. Just bring enough gun, enough water for the dog, and enough game vest for 15 collective pounds of bird.

Early in the fall sage grouse are not too tough to kill, even the big roosters which average 5 to 6 pounds. This is partly because they hold pretty close, preferring the shade of tall sagebrush to the heat of the high plains sun. As noted earlier, I've killed September sage hens with the 28-gauge at ranges up to 30 yards. They're so big that even $3/4$ of an ounce of #6's has enough pattern density at that range. I've also killed a bunch with the 20-gauge, and the 3-inch shell works even at 40 yards.

But by October things change. The young birds grow bigger, the green grass between the sagebrush has withered, and the birds are more shot-resistant. So you're shooting at tougher birds rising farther out. Unless shooting 3-inch magnums with #5's or #4's, a 20-gauge is out of its league here, especially on mature roosters at more than 35 yards. You can get some fairly close shooting on really warm days even at this time of year, but I'd carry at least a 20-gauge magnum.

A month later, forget anything smaller than the 12-gauge. While not many people hunt sage grouse at all, even fewer hunt them in November. Hunters this time of year are mostly deer hunters who run across a bunch while driving the back roads. Like sharp-tails and prairie chickens, sage hens migrate to the ridge tops at this time of year, and gather into bigger bunches. Often these aren't all crowded together like sharp-tails, perhaps because sage grouse blend more perfectly with their cover, but a long ridge will often contain loosely associated coveys of several birds. Two or three shots at one end of the ridge will send the big birds up in waves, as far along the olive-drab ridge top as you can see.

Late one October I informally guided a doctor from Washington state, a friend of a friend who wanted a couple of sage birds to mount and add to his collection. He shot an 870 Remington even older than mine, and as we unloaded the vehicles gave a long discourse on all the birds, from pheasants to ducks and geese, he'd killed with it over the years. I nodded and smiled while he told these stories, the black Lab running around the short sage next to the road getting the yips out. When the doctor was ready I whistled up the dog and we headed out. Maybe 150 yards up a big wide draw a large portion of the sage unfolded and flew into the air. The doctor shot very quickly and missed. This is possible even on sage grouse, especially the first time you see them rise. It's the same optical illusion that geese provide to the teal hunter: They seem so big and slow that you really don't have to lead them much at all. But I once flushed sage grouse and Huns from the same ridge and, while the Huns took off much more quickly, by the time the sage birds leveled off and caught the wind they passed the partridge as if they were meadowlarks—slow meadowlarks.

So the first shot missed, and the second never came, because the doctor had jammed his trusty old 870 tight. Fifty rising birds the size of young turkeys can do that. But we hunted up the scattered birds and got a few up within decent range, and he got his mounting pair. But a few at longer range shook off a $1\frac{1}{4}$-ounce load of #5's just like a goose shakes off duck loads. You could hear the shot rattle along their sides like raindrops through maple leaves.

It was one of the years when sage grouse were everywhere, and I wanted one last hunt before the seasons ended. This didn't happen until a cool day a week into November, when I knew the birds would be up on the ridge tops and pretty wild. This time I brought my own 870 and box of leftover goose loads from the lead-shot days, holding $1\frac{5}{8}$ ounces of #2 shot. Eileen parked in our favorite place along one end of a long ridge above Antelope Creek and started out. Within 100 yards we put up sage grouse, and the goose loads worked just swell. One big rooster took a shot going directly away at 50 yards and dropped like a 15-yard quail to a 28-gauge.

I had a similar experience just this last fall in the same area, but with Bismuth #2's. It was a little earlier in the year, and earlier in the morning, before the sun's warmth could settle the grouse into the shade. A half-mile from a ranch road I'd seen a bunch of Canada geese on a stock pond, and made the big sneak with the 870, loaded with 3-inch shells. When I got close to the pond there wasn't any cover along the shore, typical for a fall pond, and some of the geese were standing on the dam, making it impossible to crawl up the draw below the dam and rise up shooting. So I said to heck with it and started back toward the truck.

And that's when the sage grouse got up, a dozen birds rising raggedly like balloons let loose from a half-time celebration. They were a long way off but seemed possible, considering the goose gun. The first shot missed, but a crossing bird dropped on the second shot. Then a final bird got up even closer and flew straight away. It fell too. I paced off the shot to the far bird, the old brown Labrador snuffling through the dewy sage like a much smarter rhinoceros, and counted 55 steps. That is not untypical for a late-season sage grouse shot, and #6's or even #4's do not quite carry the mail that far, especially on a big old rooster whose skin takes some effort to puncture with a sharp hunting knife.

In most years sage grouse hunting takes some serious walking. I have dragged a couple of friends 10 miles and never seen one. This would seem to imply the use of a light shotgun, and indeed one will work just fine early in the season. But the late birds require real reach, which is pretty difficult to provide in anything less than a 12-gauge weighing at least 7 pounds. I have carried my old Model 97 Winchester and 870 Remington more miles after sage grouse than any other guns, just because they have both the power and the weight to swing and kill birds at 50 yards or more. Both weigh more than $7^1/_2$ pounds empty, but a sling helps, and there seems to be something exactly right about shooting sage grouse with an old 97.

I would love to tell more stories, like the time we stood at sunset on a ridge above Give Up Morgan Creek in late September and saw the sharp-tails flying down the side draws to water, like mountain streams flowing down to the big river. Or that day in Idaho when Steve Hughes and I went after the chukars in the deep canyon, finally shot one each after chasing them through the rocks for an hour, then ran into the big covey on our way back across the canyon and missed completely four times at 35 yards. Or the year the Huns were so thick that Eileen and I put up three coveys in a half-mile walk across a stubble field in the Judith Basin—and then walked back toward the pickup, two limits in our vests, and put up two more coveys.

But this is about shotguns, not the birds or the days. So bring a light little shotgun early on, probably with some #6 shot because, unless you hunt Huns exclusively, smaller shot does not work so well. Later on carry a 12-gauge, and some #4's and #2's along with the #6's, and some extra choke tubes. Tuck a sling into the bird vest, and get ready to see some country. Pretty soon you'll collect your own stories, and birds and days.

Late in the season sage grouse move to ridgetops and flush at longer ranges. Leave the little guns at home because November birds can be almost as tough to kill as geese.

For short-range waterfowling a classic double can be the best choice. This Mississippi mallard hunter chose a 12-gauge side-by-side for hunting the flooded timber.

CHAPTER TEN

DUCKS AND GEESE

Years ago we used to open waterfowl season in the gentle glacial prairie of the Flathead Valley, underneath the Mission Mountains, which hold their grizzly-filled heads like a less gaudy version of the Tetons over the farms and ranches below. A medium-sized reservoir near the foothills held lots of birds, and that's where most people went, waiting behind the dam and trying to pass-shoot geese as they left the lake to feed in the nearby barley and wheat fields. Some would walk the marshy edges of the lake, hoping to jump ducks from little coves.

We'd arrive in the dark, driving the road over the dam. We'd pass the pale faces of expectant goose shooters in the headlights, staring wide-eyed at us as they sat just off the edge of the road, then park at a picnic area at the far end of the dam. But instead of hunting the lake, we'd carry a bag of decoys a half-mile out on the prairie below the dam. There, 10,000 years ago, the uneven bottom of the melting glacier had left the surface of the earth slightly rumpled, like a blanket hastily thrown over a bed. The low places of this green blanket were blue, filled by water seeping through the loose soil: cattail- and rosebush-bordered ponds no more than an acre or two in size.

Ducks bred and fed and lived on these ponds, and when the mass of camouflaged humanity started shooting at the birds on the lake, many escaped to the ponds. We'd throw out a dozen decoys and wait for ducks searching for a quieter harbor. The birds were mostly blue-wing teal, mixed with a few green-wings and cinnamons, along with other occasional puddle ducks: mallards, widgeon, shovelers, once in a great while a gadwall or pintail. Sometimes even a goose would arrive, but mostly it was a teal shoot.

This was many years ago, when you could still shoot ducks with lead shot. The teal would come twisting over the decoys, occasionally plopping right in but more often zipping by like a flock of indecisive, blue-winged bats. You had to be quick, and my gun of choice back then was a Stevens side-by-side chambered for the 20-gauge magnum. It had started out in life with 28-inch barrels choked modified and full, and with a birch "walnut-stained" stock that seemed to be loosely converted from a 2×4. Even back then I was fundamentally dissatisfied with factory guns, and took a wood rasp to the stock and a hacksaw to the barrels, cutting them back half-an-inch, which opened the chokes to almost none and modified. The stock lost its pistol grip, and while you could still hold onto the forend, it didn't feel like a 2×4 anymore. Despite its low beginnings, the little gun only weighed 6½ pounds, fit me pretty well, and handled like lightning.

When a flock of teal would twist over the blocks I'd swing quickly and let fly with a 3-inch load of #7½ shot, and often a bird would fall. By the time I got on them again they'd be going away and the tighter barrel sometimes caught another bird. When bigger ducks came in I'd just wait until they were nice and close, and try to shoot them in the head. Since the season opened about the first of October, the mallards weren't laden with fat or covered with thick down, and the small shot did fine at the typically close ranges. Those of us who could shoot well had a seven-bird limit by 9 or 10 a.m. and those that weren't quite so comfortable with a scattergun still usually ended up with two or three birds.

Meanwhile the boys over at the dam would be whacking away at every goose that flew closer than rifle range. This was classic skybusting, somebody always opening up at really long range, afraid the other gunners would shoot first. By the time we left at mid-morning, the average goose-shot was probably 100 yards, and an awful lot of the loads held buckshot. I cannot recall more than one or two geese falling each year along the firing line. Once in a while we'd be resting at the picnic area, eating a sandwich before heading home, and a goose "hunter" or two would drive by and ask how we did. When we showed them our ducks they'd sometimes sneer, implying that if somebody wanted to hunt those little bitty teal it would be easy.

Retrieving a mallard on a Mississippi morning.

I don't know about you, but to me a half-dozen teal beat no goose just as often as a full house beats a straight.

Those are the extremes of waterfowling, teal and geese. So the guns and loads must be varied. Still, when somebody says "duck gun" they most often mean a 12-gauge chambered for the 3-inch magnum—or these days, the 3^1/$_2$-inch magnum.

As an all-around waterfowl piece you can't beat a relatively heavy 12-gauge, whether it's a double or a repeater. The weight can be anything from 7 pounds up, but most come in between 7^1/$_2$ and 8. That's a good weight for hunting from big-water blinds or pass-shooting, because you won't be carrying the thing too far. But for early teal, or wood ducks in the timber, or jump-shooting mallards along a prairie creek, I'll take something lighter any time. That cheap little Stevens disappeared quite a few years ago, but my much finer Beretta 16-gauge duplicates it almost exactly: a little

over 6^1/$_2$ pounds, two triggers, 27^1/$_2$-inch barrels, choked very open and medium tight. With the miracle of Bismuth it works just as well as the Stevens did, though since you can't buy Bismuth factory loads in any shot size smaller than #5, I handload it with #7's or #6's, depending on whether it's a teal shoot, or I'm jumping mallards and pheasants along a brushy stream.

The classic 12-gauge duck load was for decades a high-velocity 1^1/$_4$-ounce load, usually of #4 shot. In the old days, lots of experienced hunters and some scientific tests said that lead #4's killed big ducks more cleanly than do #6's, and when using lead-equivalent non-toxics for pass-shooting or decoy hunting I generally still use #4's, or the equivalent steel load of 1^1/$_4$ ounces of #3 or #2.

But when jump-shooting, you're mostly shooting at departing ducks. Here I like #6 Bismuth, even for big mallards. Unlike pheasants, mallards are actually eas-

The all-around duck gun has always been a 12-gauge repeater, like the pumpgun chosen by this big-water hunter.

Hand-carved diver decoys on a Montana lake.

Rosy-billed pochards in the Parana River swamps, Argentina.

A December morning on a mallard creek.

ier to kill when shot from behind than from the side, especially as the fall progresses. Early-season birds don't have the fat and down of late-fall ducks. As the season progresses the birds add more fat, more feathers, and the breast muscles toughen up with 1,000 miles of migration. At that stage of the game it's hard to drive lead-equivalent shot smaller than #4 or maybe #5 through the front of a big greenhead to the vitals.

But shoot the same bird going away and #6's work fine. Even big ducks don't have the wide, heavy pelvis of pheasants. After all, ducks don't run, and pheasants do. And when ducks spring up from a cattailed creek or high-banked irrigation ditch, they rise with heads held high on their long necks. So back-shooting with #6's works, and the smaller shot makes killing any upland birds kicked up along the way much more certain.

When using steel, #4 shot works for jump-shooting at close range, say less than 30 yards. My friend John Haviland uses his 16-gauge a lot for this kind of work.

Down in Alabama, Bo Pitman likes to hunt wood ducks on the timbered ponds of White Oak Plantation with a 20-gauge and steel shot. But shooting steel in any gauge less than 12 takes more discipline and skill than most of us possess. I would rather load one of the softer non-toxics and shoot one of my side-by-sides. Bismuth does the job in open-choked guns, but even a tightly-choked old Parker or L.C. Smith should work quite well when loaded with the faster-spreading Federal Tungsten-Polymer shells.

The same sort of gun works pretty well on decoying puddle ducks, especially at the close ranges of timber shooting. Last winter down in Mississippi my old Fox double was just about perfect with #4 Bismuth when shooting mallards and gadwalls under the flooded oaks along the levees. You usually won't get more than two shots in this hunting, and two chokes definitely help. It would have worked equally well with Tungsten-Polymer #6's, which I'd choose over the #4's for close work, since they spread more quickly and penetrate just a little deeper than the same size of Bismuth. If shooting steel in the same conditions I'd take #3's, with a loose improved cylinder choke. The .006-inch tube in my old 870 pumpgun is ideal.

On more open water most people carry bigger guns, especially if they shoot steel. There is nothing quite like a pumpgun or rugged autoloader for most of this work. Before soft non-toxics I shot my old 870 at more ducks than any other shotgun. Today's steel loads work far better than the early stuff, and with a 3-inch load of steel #2's even tough diving ducks can be taken at 40 yards or a little more. On the rare occasions I hunt divers the 870 still gets chosen, these days with a 28" barrel designed for steel shot. I don't always shoot steel—$1^3/_8$ ounces of #4 Bismuth or hard tungsten works better than even the best steel loads—but the heavier weight of the steel-proof barrel helps keep the gun swinging. Diving ducks over a big decoy spread often just fly fast past the spread and even when shot at don't flare like puddle ducks. You need a shotgun with some reach and some weight forward to keep that barrel moving out in front of 50-mile-per-hour birds.

Screw-in chokes have done wonders for waterfowl guns. Today's tighter-shooting loads of steel, hard tungsten and even Bismuth indicate modified choke for most duck

The same guns and loads that work for long-range ducks also work for the smaller geese. Here Alberta guide Nick Frederick carries a white-fronted goose back to the blind.

187

Canada geese over the Dakotas.

hunting, except perhaps long-range divers or pass-shooting of big mallards; but on windy days screwing in an improved-modified choke really helps. Good waterfowling is normally a breezy undertaking and a really hard wind tends to open patterns. Even shooting mallards over decoys requires more choke when gusts of 30 miles per hour are trying to take the top off the lake. In steel, the $3^1/_2$-inch 12-gauge or 10-gauge loaded with #2 shot is about the best you can shoot on windy days. In Bismuth, the old standby high-velocity duck load of $1^1/_4$ ounces of #4 works fine, but wind is one place where hard tungsten shot really shines, since it patterns tighter and seems to cut through the wind better than anything else. Just use the heaviest, standard-velocity loads of #4 shot that will fit in your gun, and forget the other shot sizes. They simply don't have enough pattern density, especially in the wind.

The same guns and loads will work on smaller geese, from mallard-sized brant to the wide variety of geese weighing from 5 to 7 pounds, whether snows or blues or lesser Canadas. While these can be twice the size of a big mallard, they really don't take much more penetration, and their bigger vital area means more shot hits the bird. Several years ago Eileen and I hunted lesser Canadas, mixed with a few snows, up in Alberta with Edmonton outfitter Pat Frederick and his son Nick. It was two years before Canada banned lead. Over the three-day hunt, we found that traditional honker loads

Modern non-toxic shot works better in very open chokes when shooting over decoys.

with #2 shot had too little pattern for these smaller geese, even the lesser Canadas. Heavy duck loads with #4 lead worked far better, and when I go up again (hopefully soon), I'll take the same load in Bismuth or hard tungsten, or $3\frac{1}{2}$-inch magnum 12s loaded with #2 steel. If you ever get a chance to hunt geese in the prairie provinces of Canada. It's worth it, even with that gun-registration charge they impose at the border these days. (Hey, it's 50 bucks *Canadian*, barely the price of a tank of gas.) Limits are typically at least a dozen geese a day.

For big Canadas I just won't use steel in anything less than a $3\frac{1}{2}$-inch 12-gauge, and I use that at less than 50 yards. It takes at least a BB steel pellet to equal the penetration of a #2 Bismuth or #4 hard tungsten at ranges under 40 yards, and a BBB to match them at 50. Even the biggest $3\frac{1}{2}$-inch 12- or 10-gauge steel loads won't consistently kill big geese past 50 yards. They pattern very tightly, and you'll have goose-killing density in the middle of the pattern. But there just aren't enough of the big shot, even in a 10-gauge shell.

Let's go back to our pattern-density formula. A 12-pound Canada goose has a vital area of about 40 square inches, depending on which way he's facing. A $1\frac{7}{8}$-ounce load of Bismuth #2's (available in $3\frac{1}{2}$-inch 12- and 10-gauge shells) contains about 160 pellets, and a full-choke gun will often put half of those in a 30-inch circle at 60 yards. Some chokes will do the same at 70 yards. That's one shot pellet every 8.75 square inches, which means four or five hits on a big goose.

The same $3\frac{1}{2}$-inch shells will hold $1\frac{3}{8}$ ounces of steel. With BBB's, that's only 84 pellets in the whole load. The best pattern I obtained from any gun in either 12- or 10-gauge only put 58 shot in a 30-inch circle at 50 yards. That's a 69 percent pattern, a very good percentage at 50 yards, and adequate for consistent goose killing. But remember, that was the *best* pattern; most placed about 50 BBB's in the 30-inch circle at that range.

While BB's show more pattern density, they just don't penetrate like BBB's—or Bismuth or hard tungsten #2's, or even hard tungsten #4's. So 50 yards is

Steel shot brought back the 10-gauge, and there's still no finer choice for really big geese at long range. Many hunters use autoloaders like this Remington SP-10 to take some of the sting out of big shells.

A few long-range goose hunters mount non-magnifying optical sights like the Bushnell Holosight on their shotguns, which helps precise aiming past 40 yards.

about the limit for shooting Canada geese with the very biggest steel loads. With 3-inch shells the maximum range would be closer yet, about 40 to 45 yards.

Of course, you could quite validly argue that damn few hunters are capable of consistently hitting any gamebird much past 40 yards, and some of us are done before that. That's true, but the denser patterns of Bismuth and hard tungsten allow more leeway, both in range estimation and hits around the fringes. Big steel shot patterns so tightly that the fringe of a 30-inch pattern is often very thin even at 40 yards.

Yeah, Bismuth and tungsten cost around twice as much, but how many Canada geese do we shoot a year? Five or six? Even if we only kill a third of the birds we shoot at, 20 rounds should take care of a season. If you insist, keep hunting big Canadas with steel, but I can certainly spring for 20 rounds of Bismuth or tungsten a year. Even if we take 15 birds on a Cana-

dian hunt, that's still less than 50 shells, if we shoot halfway competently. Most of us shoot geese too infrequently to get really good at it, and can use the help the denser patterns Bismuth or hard tungsten provide.

If those alternatives to steel continue to grow more popular, I suspect the 10-gauge may start fading away again. Because Bismuth and hard tungsten pattern so well, there's little difference in performance between the $3^1/_2$-inch 12-gauge and the 10, especially when many $3^1/_2$-inch 12s come from the factory overbored these days. To tell the truth, I wouldn't bet on which shell I'm holding in my hand, unless allowed to cheat by looking at the headstamp. Why shoot an 11-pound 10-gauge when something like the Browning Gold takes so much sting out of the $3^1/_2$-inch 12, in a gun that weighs less than 8 pounds? Instead of a pure goose gun, shooters can buy something equally useful on sporting clays, pheasants or decoyed mallards. I ad-

These Western goose hunters are shooting autoloaders in 12- and 10-gauge magnum. Modern non-toxic shot like Bismuth and tungsten has made the 3-inch 12 an effective choice for Canada geese again.

mire the big 10-gauge autoloaders produced by Browning and Remington, but the real reason for their existence is steel shot. As better solutions keep making their way into waterfowl loads, the days of the big autoloaders may be numbered.

You can buy pumps, doubles and even bolt-actions for the big loads, but my one pumpgun experience with the 3½-inch 12-gauge took place over 10 years ago at a writer's conference in Utah. Mossberg had a few of their new pumpguns chambered for the super 12 at a skeet range, of all things. I shot one three times, if memory serves, until finding the right swing from station 4, and that was enough to last me a lifetime. I have shot "elephant rifles" in calibers up to .505 Gibbs and never been kicked harder. While some part of me yearns for a big 10-gauge double, 25-year-old experiences with my friend Norm Strung's big AyA have kept the Visa card in my pocket whenever I find one of the things. In anything except a gas-operated autoloader, the really big shells simply kick too much for most humans.

But the miracle of

There's nothing in wingshooting to match carrying a big Canada goose back to the blind. This shooter chose a 3-inch 12-gauge with bismuth 2's.

Packing out some January greenheads in Mississippi.

197

Mallard hunting in the flooded timber along the Mississippi River.

Waiting for incomers in flooded timber.

the new soft non-toxics does allow us to use older guns, especially on lighter waterfowl than Canada geese. For some waterfowl hunters, old shotguns hold the same attractions they do for upland hunting. Old guns, like drams-equivalent and wooden duck calls and hand-carved decoys, connect us to the hunters who waded the marshes before us.

Last winter on the lower Mississippi River a bunch of us brought old doubles and 97 Winchester pump-guns to hunt the standing timber. We even wore Filson waxed-canvas duck coats and hats, though I will admit that on the second day, when a hard cold front blew through, many of us wore Polarfleece and Gore-Tex under the canvas.

But it felt great, standing under the trees and seeing the ducks filter down through the branches, hearing oil-finished walnut whisper against canvas as we raised the old guns. And the mallards and wood ducks fell just as cleanly as they would to any modern autoloader, to shots fired from guns that were brand new back when heath hens still danced in the spring meadows of Massachusetts, and humanity had never seen a World War.

It felt just as good to come into the cabin at night, to wipe the muddy guns down and place them gently on the rack in the front hall, where wet canvas had been hung up to dry. Often we'd stand in there, still cold but warming from both outside and inside, both from the fire and some brown liquid, whiskey or coffee, and think of the way the birds flew. There is hunting, and then there is wingshooting, and then we remember.

Quitting time in the flooded timber.

Labrador at the gates of dawn.

BIBLIOGRAPHY

BOOKS

Askins, Charles. *Game Bird Shooting.* New York: The MacMillan Company, 1931.

Bodio, Stephen (editor). *The Art of Shooting Flying.* South Hamilton, Massachusetts: GSJ Press, 1988.

Bodio, Stephen. *Good Guns.* New York: Nick Lyons Books, 1986.

Boothroyd, Geoffrey. *The Shotgun, History and Development.* Long Beach, California: Safari Press, 1985.

Brister, Bob. Shotgunning, *The Art and the Science.* Piscataway, New Jersey: New Century Publishers (Winchester Press), 1976.

Butler, David F. *The American Shotgun.* Middlefield, Connecticut: Lyman Publications, 1973.

Cadieux, Charles L. *Successful Goose Hunting.* Washington, D.C.: Stone Wall Press, Inc., 1986.

Curtis, Capt. Paul A. *Guns and Gunning.* Philadelphia: The Penn Publishing Co.,1934.

Fackler, Kurt D. and M.L. McPherson. *Reloading For Shotgunners*, 4th Edition. Iola, Wisconsin, Krause Publications, 1997.

Fergus, Charles. *The Upland Equation.* New York: Lyons & Burford, 1995.

Fergus, Jim. *A Hunter's Road.* New York: Henry Holt and Company, Inc., 1992.

Garwood, G.T. *Gough Thomas's Gun Book.* New York: Winchester Press, 1972.

Greener, W.W. *The Gun and its Development.* Secaucus, New Jersey: Chartwell Books, Inc., 1988.

Grooms, Steve. *Modern Pheasant Hunting.* Harrisburg, Pennsylvania: Stackpole Books, 1982.

Grooms, Steve. *Pheasant Hunter's Harvest.* New York: Lyons & Burdford, 1990.

Grozik, Richard S. *Game Gun.* Traverse City, Michigan: Countrysport Press, 1997.

Hill, Gene. *A Shotgunner's Notebook.* New Albany, Ohio: Countrysport Press, 1989.

Hochbaum, H. Albert. *Travels and Traditions of Waterfowl.* Newton, Massachusetts: Charles T. Branford Co., 1955.

Huggler, Tom. *Grouse of North America.* Minocqua, Wisconsin: Willow Creek Press, 1990.

Hughes, Steven Dodd. *Fine Gunmaking: Double Shotguns.* Iola, Wisconsin: Krause Publications, 1998.

Johnson, Peter H. Parker, *America's Finest Shotgun.* New York: Bonanza Books, 1961

Keith, Elmer. *Shotguns by Keith.* Harrisburg, Pennsylvania: Stackpole & Heck, Inc, 1950.

McIntosh, Michael. *Shotguns and Shooting.* Selma, Alabama: Countrysport Press, 1995.

McIntyre, Thomas. *The Way of the Hunter.* New York: E.P. Dutton, 1988.

Moreton, Dave (editor). *Gun Talk.* New York: Winchester Press, 1973.

O'Connor, Jack. *The Shotgun Book.* New York: Alfred A. Knopf, 1965.

Petzal, David E. (editor). *The Encyclopedia of Sporting Firearms.* New York: Facts On File, Inc., 1991.

Petzal, David E. (editor). *The Experts Book of the Shooting Sports.* New York: Simon and Schuster, 1972.

Proper, Datus C. *Pheasants of the Mind*. New York: Prentice Hall Press, 1990.

Reiger, George. *The Wings of Dawn*. New York: Nick Lyons Books, 1980.

Reiger, George. *The Wildfowler's Quest*. New York: Lyons & Burford, 1989.

Rue, Leonard Lee III. *Game Birds of North America*. New York: Harper & Row, 1973.

Strung, Norman. *Misty Mornings and Moonless Nights, A Waterfowler's Guide*. New York, Macmillan Publishing Co., 1974.

Tate, Douglas. Birmingham Gunmakers. Long Beach, California: Safari Press, 1997.

Trueblood, Ted. The Ted Trueblood Hunting Treasury. New York: David McKay Company, Inc., 1978.

Waterman, Charles F. *Hunting Upland Birds*. South Hackensack, New Jersey: Stoeger Publishing Co., 1972.

Wieland, Terry. *Spanish Best*. New Albany, Ohio: Countrysport Press, 1994.

Woolner, Frank. *Grouse and Grouse Hunting*. New York: Crown Publishers, 1970.

Yardley, Michael. *Gunfitting*. Long Beach, California: Safari Press, 1996.

Zutz, Don. *The Double Shotgun*. Clinton, New Jersey: New Win Publishing (Winchester Press), 1985.

Zutz, Don. *Grand Old Shotguns*. Auburn, California, Further Adventures, Inc., 1995.

Zutz, Don. *Shotgun Stuff*. Auburn, California: Shotgun Sports, Inc., 1991.

PERIODICALS

Double Gun Journal. East Jordan, Michigan: The Double Gun Journal, Inc.

Field & Stream. New York: Times-Mirror Magazines.

Gun Digest. Iola, Wisconsin: Krause Publications.

Outdoor Life. New York: Times Mirror Magazines.

Petersen's Shotguns. Los Angeles, California, Petersen's Publishing Co.

Shooting Sportsman. Rockport, Maine: Down East Enterprise, Inc.

Sporting Clays. San Antonio, Texas: Sporting Clays, Ltd.

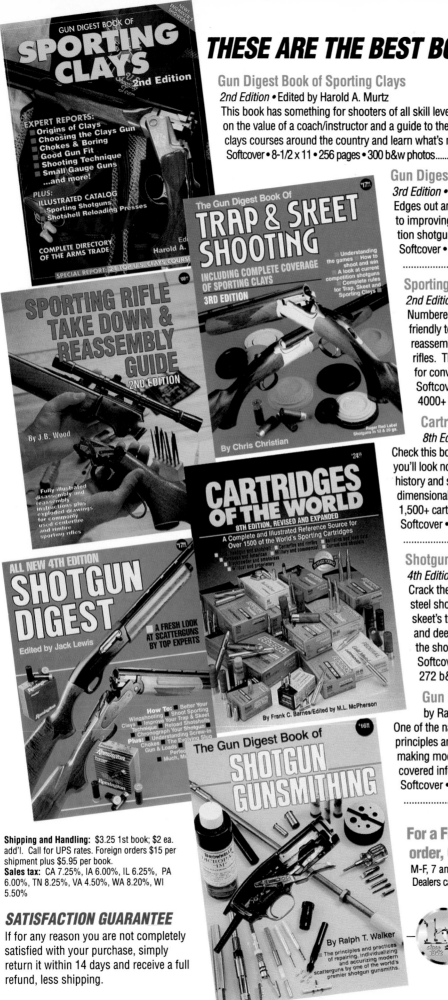

THESE ARE THE BEST BOOKS FOR SHOOTERS

Gun Digest Book of Sporting Clays
2nd Edition • Edited by Harold A. Murtz
This book has something for shooters of all skill levels, including tips for new shooters, a discussion on the value of a coach/instructor and a guide to the best training for young shooters. Take a tour of clays courses around the country and learn what's new in guns, gear and ammunition.
Softcover • 8-1/2 x 11 • 256 pages • 300 b&w photos..................SC2 • $21.95

Gun Digest Book of Trap & Skeet Shooting
3rd Edition • by Chris Christian
Edges out any other guide! Speaks to any shooter dedicated to improving scores or simply enjoying the sport. Competition shotguns, complete rules included.
Softcover • 8-1/4 x 10-11/16 • 288 pages • 325 b&w photos
....TS3 • $17.95

Sporting Rifle Take Down & Reassembly Guide
2nd Edition • by J.B. Wood
Numbered, exploded or isometric drawings and user-friendly text explain each step of the takedown and reassembly process for 52 popular centerfire and rimfire rifles. This "must-have" reference includes labeled parts for convenient reference. More than 2,000 b&w photos.
Softcover • 8-1/4 x 10-11/16 • 480 pages
4000+ b&w photos .... SRAT • $19.95

Cartridges of the World
8th Edition • by Frank Barnes; M. L. McPherson, Editor
Check this book first for answers to cartridge ID questions and you'll look no further. This new 8th edition unfolds cartridge history and spotlights recommended uses. Detailed photos, dimensional drawings, loading data, and ballistics charts for 1,500+ cartridges complete the package.
Softcover • 8-1/4 x 10-11/16 • 480 pages • 450 b&w photos
....COW8 • $24.95

Shotgun Digest
4th Edition • by Jack Lewis
Crack the case on the latest in guns and loads, including steel shot. Check out the basics of sporting clays. Master skeet's toughest shots. Then move on to wingshooting and deer and upland game hunting. Jack Lewis explains the shotgun as a self-defense weapon.
Softcover • 8-1/4 x 10-11/16 • 256 pages
272 b&w photos .... SD4 • $17.95

Gun Digest Book of Shotgun Gunsmithing
by Ralph T. Walker
One of the nation's premier shotgun specialists explains the principles and practices of repairing, individualizing and making modern scatter-guns more accurate. Never-before covered information!
Softcover • 8-1/2 x 11 • 256 pages • 410 b&w photos
....SHSM • $16.95

Shipping and Handling: $3.25 1st book; $2 ea. add'l. Call for UPS rates. Foreign orders $15 per shipment plus $5.95 per book.
Sales tax: CA 7.25%, IA 6.00%, IL 6.25%, PA 6.00%, TN 8.25%, VA 4.50%, WA 8.20%, WI 5.50%

SATISFACTION GUARANTEE
If for any reason you are not completely satisfied with your purchase, simply return it within 14 days and receive a full refund, less shipping.

For a FREE catalog or to place a credit card order, Call 800-258-0929 Dept. GNB9

M-F, 7 am - 8 pm • Sat, 8 am - 2 pm, CST
Dealers call toll-free 888-457-2873 ext 880, M-F, 8 am - 5 pm

krause publications
700 E State St, Iola, WI 54990
Visit and order from our secure web site: www.krausebooks.com

BOOKS THE EXPERTS DEPEND ON

Fine Gunmaking: Double Shotguns

by Steven Dodd Hughes

An in-depth look at what goes into creating some of the world's finest custom shotguns. One of the top custom gunmakers in the United States invites you into his shop, giving you a feel for the craftsmanship and detail that goes into a truly great shotgun.

Hardcover • 8-1/2 x 11 • 160 pages • 63 b&w photos • 53 color photos .... **FGDS • $34.95**

The Winchester Model 52

Perfection In Design • by Herbert G. Houze

Historical arms enthusiast Herbert Houze unravels the mysteries surrounding the development of what many consider the most perfect rifle ever made. Covers the rifle's improvements through five modifications. Users, collectors and marksmen will appreciate each history, serial number sequences and authentic photos.

Hardcover • 8-1/2 x 11 • 192 pages • 190 b&w photos
....**WIN • $34.95**

Browning Superposed

John M. Browning's Last Legacy • by Ned Schwing

Chronicles the history of North America's best-selling over and under gun. Offers serial numbers, sales figures and total number sold by gauge with rare photos and official company records.

Hardcover/jacket • 8-1/2 x 11 • 496 pages • 550 b&w photos 100 color photos.. **FBS01 • $49.95**

Remington Firearms: The Golden Age of Collecting

by Robert W.D. Ball

Comprehensive pictorial history of Remington through World War I. Brings you never-before-seen pictures of the legendary Moldenhauer collection, profiles of more than 400 guns with historical insights, illustrations and value guide.

Hardcover • 8-1/2 x 11 • 194 pages • 150 b&w photos
....**GAR01 • $29.95**

Modern Custom Guns

Walnut, Steel, and Uncommon Artistry • by Tom Turpin

Rifles, shotguns and handguns from today's most talented artists are discussed in fine detail in this handsome hardcover volume. From exquisite engraving to the beauty of exotic woods, the mystique of today's custom guns is expertly detailed. Includes full-color photos of many of the world's most beautiful firearms.

Hardcover • 8-1/2 x 11 • 208 pages • 225 color photos
.... **MCG01 • $49.95**

Gun Digest 2000

54th Edition • Edited by Ken Warner

The most comprehensive annual book on shooting sports. This new edition is filled with fresh articles from firearms experts and scholars. The latest prices and specifications on more than 3,000 currently available firearms from the US and around the world, as well as handloading presses, optics and ammunition. The freshly updated Directory of the Arms Trade provides the detail necessary to contact any business that is active in the shooting sports industry.

Softcover • 8-1/2 x 11 • 544 pages • 2,300+ b&w photos
....**GD2000 • $24.95**

For a FREE catalog or to place a credit card order, Call 800-258-0929   Dept. GNB9
M-F, 7 am - 8 pm • Sat, 8 am - 2 pm, CST
Dealers call toll-free 888-457-2873 ext 880, M-F, 8 am - 5 pm

 **krause publications**

700 E State St, Iola, WI 54990
Visit and order from our secure web site:
www.krausebooks.com